Laura Haycock begins this book by sayi[ng that to]
organizations support women better in [menopause, she has]
knocked it out of the park! *M-POWER* [is wonderfully]
written and chock-full of evidence-based [guidance.]
It features brilliant case studies from me[n and women]
of all different shapes and sizes. The book is also very nuanced, paying
careful attention to gender inclusivity and intersectionality. Perhaps even
more importantly, the M-POWERED framework is easy to remember as
well as comprehensive and sensible. I thoroughly enjoyed reading this
book and recommend it very highly indeed to anyone (business leaders
in particular) who wants to understand more about how to support
menopausal staff at work, and why this is so important. Brava, Laura, and
I mean that very sincerely indeed!

Professor Jo Brewis
Co-author of the UK Government report *The Effects of Menopause Transition on Women's Economic Participation in the UK* and co-editor of *Menopause Transitions in the Workplace*

Menopause and hormonal changes are still often misunderstood and underestimated, especially in the workplace. Many people are confused how best to help women who are experiencing symptoms, and this book will help provide clarity. Any organization who employs women should have ready access to this book.

Dr. Louise Newson
Founder of Newson Health Group, and member of the UK Government's Menopause Taskforce. Award-winning educator, podcaster, and author of *The Definitive Guide to the Perimenopause and Menopause*

Laura's book makes a persuasive case for implementing a menopause action plan, emphasizing its strategic value for businesses. With the rise of older women in the workforce and evidence of a menopause penalty, the book underscores the urgent need to support women – and businesses – in reaching their full potential. Backed by insights from social research, medicine, law and organizational science, it builds a compelling argument for change. The second half introduces the M-POWERED framework, offering adaptable, practical steps for organizations. A must-read for business leaders seeking a clear and practical guide on this critical issue.

Max Landsberg
Bestselling author of *The Tao of Coaching*, former Partner at McKinsey & Co, and Heidrick & Struggles

I loved this book and will be gifting it to multiple clients. So much has been written about the menopause, but business leaders are still craving a down-to-earth approach that gets to the heart of what they can do to enable their female talent to progress and thrive through the menopause years. Leaders will particularly value the M-POWERED framework. In clear language, it sets out how you can deliver on a menopause policy (rather than write it and ignore it!), helping the reader with tools such as how to develop a business case, estimate ROI, maintain relationships and develop a good strategy. Illustrated with case studies throughout, this is an invaluable read for anyone interested in retaining the women in their business.

Lucy Ryan
Managing Director, Mindspring; Author of award-winning
Revolting Women: Why midlife women walk out and what to do about it

This groundbreaking book is a much-needed wake-up call for business leaders to step up and support the women who power their organizations. The UK is leading the charge on the global stage, and Laura Haycock delivers a compelling business case for why menopause-friendly workplaces aren't just a nice-to-have – they're essential for future-proofing your talent strategy. The M-POWERED Framework is particularly valuable, offering a clear, practical and actionable approach that is both smart and necessary. This book isn't just about making businesses better – it's about creating truly inclusive workplaces where everyone can thrive. If you're serious about retaining top talent and driving real change, this is your go-to guide. After all, thriving businesses start with thriving people – and that includes women at every stage of life.

Heidi Cooper
Employment Lawyer at HCR Law, Independent Panel
member for The Menopause Friendly Accreditation

M-POWER is a must read for business leaders who want to create a truly inclusive workplace. Too often menopause is ignored or misunderstood but this book cuts through the stigma and harmful myths with clarity, compassion and evidence-based insights. The M-POWERED framework provides a clear, practical road map for organizations to become menopause friendly ensuring that employees feel supported, valued and empowered at every stage in their careers. With an engaging style, practical strategies, and compelling case studies, this book equips leaders with the knowledge and confidence to support employees through this transition. Forward-thinking organizations that embrace a menopause-friendly people strategy will gain a competitive edge in attracting and retaining top talent. An essential guide for any leader committed to building a high-performing, inclusive workplace.

Joanne Healy
Head of Group Employee Relations, Bank of Ireland,
Qualified Barrister, and Co-author of *Human Resources
and Employment: Policies and procedures*

I found this an excellent and empowering read, inviting the reader to join the discussion in an accessible and relaxed style. It made the point very strongly that there is a 'menopause penalty' that society needs to recognize and address. This comes at a timely point given the growing political activity around menopause, in addition to the significant interest from women themselves. I would recommend this book to women in work, organizations and managers to ensure we all recognize the menopausal workforce phenomenon, and so that we work together to retain the valuable contribution this group provides.

Jacqui McBurnie
NENC ICB Menopause Lead; Founder and former Chair of the Menopause Network, member of the Cross-Government Menopause Network Executive Steering Committee

Very easy to digest, with an open sanguine style that neither preaches nor self-indulges, Laura's book provides constructive clear fact-based advice for supporting working women through their menopause experience. Part 1 provides a useful summary of how and why menopause affects women, the impact it has on women's working lives, and why organizations should take action. Lots of the information was either new to me, or I hadn't seen presented in this way before. Part 2 is more focused on what organizations can do to support women. The M-POWERED framework whilst aspirational, also feels realistic and achievable, and I valued the inclusion of case studies that illustrated different approaches UK companies have taken. Definitely a must-read for anyone working in HR or talent development.

Maxine Zaidman
Associate Director at JBA Consulting,
Head of Learning Development, Marketing and Support

As a middle-aged guy and business leader, I'll admit I initially approached a book about menopause at work with a degree of hesitation. I felt I was out of my depth and wasn't quite sure how relevant it would be to me. But I couldn't have been more wrong. Laura's groundbreaking work completely changed the way I view this critical workplace issue. Laura weaves a compelling narrative that's both eye-opening and practical. She dismantles the taboos surrounding menopause with precision and empathy, shining a light on the real challenges women face and the real consequences of organizational inaction. What really sets this book apart, though, is its practical focus with a clear, actionable roadmap for change. This isn't just a book for HR leaders – it's for anyone who cares about the future of work. It will challenge your assumptions and equip you to drive meaningful change.

Craig Simpson
CEO, O.R. Talent

M-POWER is a highly practical framework supporting business leaders' understanding and approach to supporting critical valued team members at a vulnerable time, and we all know that we follow leaders who care. It goes beyond the commercial rationale for attracting and retaining talent, to leading with empathy and belonging. The book is thoroughly researched, coupled with case examples, which I really enjoyed. These provided leading practice, aspirational and inspirational company approaches and the reputational, retention and empathetic value achieved. A must read for business leaders, and those holding the policy pen, giving them the confidence to drive forward on supporting others facing these challenges in the future. For female leaders themselves, I see this book being of real benefit in helping them understand how their own experiences compare to others.

Helen Pullen
Director at Minerva Performance Consulting,
Learning and Organisational Development at NFU Mutual

The menopause has been sadly overlooked when it comes to inclusion at work. Laura's book changes all of that! Accessible and easy to read, yet packed with powerful research and real-life case studies, her book offers leaders practical tips on how to break down taboos, create a compelling argument for change, and lead with compassion and collaboration. It highlights an often-overlooked aspect of our inclusion obligations. Each stage of the M-POWERED framework offers step-by-step guidance towards creating a menopause friendly working environment. Anyone who is truly committed to helping workplaces thrive through the power of its people, *all* people, will find this an invaluable companion on the journey. Read this book!

Jon Atkins
Business Psychologist and Inclusion Specialist

This book is an invaluable resource that addresses the often-overlooked challenges faced by women going through menopause. What makes it truly unique are the easy-to-implement, actionable insights and practical strategies aimed at helping any individual or organization create and develop a menopause-friendly workplace environment that supports, empowers and inspires everyone. Specsavers are committed to fostering an inclusive and supportive workplace culture, having proactively taken steps towards achieving Menopause Friendly Accreditation. This book will help other businesses – large and small – to achieve the same.

Lou Furby
Specsavers Menopause Network Group Co-Chair

M-POWER by Laura Haycock is an important book. Menopause was rarely, if ever, discussed in companies until recently. I have to admit that menopause was never something that I considered or addressed, even when running companies with a large proportion of female employees. I wish

I had read *M-POWER*. Laura talks powerfully about her own experience, but the book also contains a goldmine of information about the physical and mental impacts of menopause. It sets out invaluable, practical guidance for leaders to make their organizations better able to support people going through menopause. Male leaders – and I deliberately say this to you as one myself – get a copy and read it as soon as you can! It will help you understand and support a large proportion of working people to get through a difficult stage of life and do their best work.

Dominic Shales
Founder, RESET Media Group

This book delivered on many levels. As a woman in her 50s there were multiple places where I internally shouted 'yes!' as it captured so many of my experiences of working through the menopause. As an educationalist I was convinced by its use of academic research to establish how significant and widespread the issue is. And as the leader of a business employing over 800 people, I found the book of enormous practical benefit. The chapter summaries and case studies helped me move from thinking 'that's interesting and important' to 'this is what we can do about it' such as achieving cultural change through implementing coaching conversations. And as a busy person juggling multiple priorities, the M-POWERED framework offered me a simple but flexible approach to making an immediate and lasting impact.

Emma Taylor
Warden/CEO Dean Close Foundation

Laura's personal story really resonated with my own and countless other women's experiences and the way the book unfolded had me hooked! Her humour brings well placed levity to a serious and important subject – the subtitles are still making me smile! – and her practical suggestions in the M-POWERED framework, based on solid science were excellent. This book is so useful for anyone who needs to and wants to know more about the impact of the menopause and is an absolute must for managers and leaders, to help navigate the unique, yet commonplace, turbulence that the menopause creates. My hope is that despite the many and varied challenges that menopausal women face daily (and nightly!), that this book helps more wonderful women feel supported, as they find ways to continue to contribute and drive value in their roles at work and in life.

Gill Graham
Principal Psychologist and Partner, Cargyll

A must read for anyone who wants to create an inclusive organization that enables women to thrive through menopause and beyond. Written at a time when the public dialogue on menopause is growing, but workplaces are slow to adapt due to a lack of practical advice, this book seeks to bridge the gap. Laura weaves together research, storytelling and practical advice, introducing the M-POWERED framework to give business leaders confidence in taking action. By the end you will feel compelled that addressing menopause in the workplace is a social, moral and business imperative, requiring strategic, inclusive and empathetic efforts. At a time when humanity is facing some of its greatest challenges, every leader must know how to tackle menopause. Laura shows us how.

Adina Uritescu
Group Head of Leadership, Talent and DEI, Direct Line Group

If you want to engage, enable and, most importantly, retain the women working in your organization, then you need to dive into this book! Laura Haycock's M-POWERED framework takes you step-by-step through everything you need to know – and do – to build a resilient work experience for those on the menopause journey. She adopts a science-led and evidence-based approach which, combined with her deep understanding of human and organizational behaviour, provides rich insights for all business leaders – and indeed anyone in the workplace. I particularly love the coaching bias, as well as the case studies and real-life examples making this a practical and pragmatic read. Laura's voice is so natural and engaging that it's an easy read (not an easy topic!) and you'll fly through the pages ready to M-POWER your organization!

Stephanie Rudbeck
Senior Talent Management, Development and Coaching Specialist, past Senior Director, Talent & Reward at Willis Towers Watson

M-POWER is an excellent business book that de-mystifies and de-stigmatizes this challenging, un-predictable, and often mis-understood life-stage. Many leaders may be yet to explore how they address this issue, despite it affecting a huge proportion of the workforce. M-POWER provides the best starting point to open up the conversation. The book is extremely well written through both a personal lens and also a unique organizational, historical and societal perspective. It is thoroughly researched and also pragmatic in content and tone, making it both thought-provoking and, ultimately, very readable. Helpful summaries at the end of each chapter reinforce the overarching themes. Key messages that resonated include the importance of empathic cultures that are psychologically safe, and of offering adaptable work environments. This book will encourage business leaders to hold up the mirror to their own practices, policies and approaches, the M-POWERED framework providing a very useful structure to achieve this.

Andrew Lawson
Experienced People Director within education and hospitality sectors and past Head of HR at Shakespeare's Globe

M-POWER
A MENOPAUSE ACTION PLAN FOR ORGANIZATIONS

LAURA HAYCOCK

First published in Great Britain by Practical Inspiration Publishing, 2025

© Laura Haycock, 2025

The moral rights of the author have been asserted

ISBN   978-1-78860-732-2   (hardback)
        978-1-78860-733-9   (paperback)
        978-1-78860-734-6   (epub)
        978-1-78860-735-3   (Kindle)

All rights reserved. This book, or any portion thereof, may not be reproduced without the express written permission of the author.

Every effort has been made to trace copyright holders and to obtain their permission for the use of copyright material. The publisher apologizes for any errors or omissions and would be grateful if notified of any corrections that should be incorporated in future reprints or editions of this book.

EU GPSR representative: LOGOS EUROPE, 9 rue Nicolas Poussin, LA ROCHELLE 17000, France Contact@logoseurope.eu

Want to bulk-buy copies of this book for your team and colleagues? We can customize the content and co-brand *M-POWER* to suit your business's needs.

Please email info@practicalinspiration.com for more details.

Contents

Preface xiii
Introduction xvii

Part 1: The case for taking action 1

1. **Time for a re-think on menopause 3**
   What's new about old women? 4
   Menopausal women have a lot going on 13
   The changing world for working women 17

2. **Understanding the menopause transition
   and its impact 25**
   All aboard the hormone roller-coaster 26
   Shaken not stirred: managing a cocktail of
   menopause symptoms 33
   How menopause puts the breaks on women at work 44
   In conclusion 47

3. **Why menopause-friendly organizations deliver
   value 49**
   Securing a strategic, financial and ethical pay-off 50
   Managing the risk of legal challenge 59

4. Focal points for change 73
   Turning taboo into 'Wow! Who knew?!' 74
   The problem ain't women! 84
   Empowerment lost and found 93

Part 2: From awareness to action 101

5. M-POWERED: a framework for creating a menopause action plan 103

6. Purpose: stakeholders engaged in a shared *purpose* 107
   Demonstrate strategic alignment 108
   Estimate the return on investment 112
   Engage stakeholders in your menopause policy commitments 114

7. Openness: courage and *openness* to talk and to learn 119
   Get the conversations started 120
   Shine a light on menopause inequity 125
   Listen to women and their experiences 127

8. Will: personal *will* and agency, in voice and choice 133
   Encourage shared decision-making 134
   Allow flexible options 137
   Know when it's ok to say 'no' 143

9. Effectiveness: ability, potential and *effectiveness* 147
   Refocus on strengths and the capacity to adapt and grow 148
   Reinforce positive role models 151
   Resolve beliefs, emotions and habits that get in the way 152

10. Relationships: supportive, trusting *relationships* and culture 157
   Develop menopause awareness and skills 158
   Reinforce a menopause-friendly culture 161
   Build and connect the community 165

11. Environment: menopause-friendly physical *environment* 171
   Keep it cool 173
   Keep it calm 175
   Keep it discrete and convenient 176
   Keep it safe 177

12. Delivery: sustainable and systemic *delivery* 183
   Start with the beginning, middle and the end in mind 184
   Establish a menopause 'golden thread' 187
   Keep an eye on progress 191

Conclusion 195

Notes 199

Useful resources 217

Acknowledgements 219

Index 223

Preface

My own experience of menopause was not plain sailing. In fact, at times, it felt like being lost in a constantly changing sea. Like most people, I had been totally ignorant of menopause. I had a vague sense that it could make women less visible or, at worst, turn them into objects of ridicule. I had no idea how it would impact my own life and career, what to look out for or what options I might have to help me manage it. I had little clue how to keep holding my head up high at work as I experienced the highs and lows of this inevitable transition.

In hindsight, I must have started perimenopause in my late 30s. I had no idea what was going on and neither did my GP. I had noticed more joint and muscle pain, more heavy bleeding, more erratic moods and chronic sleeplessness. However, by my early 40s my marriage had broken down and I was adjusting to being a single working mum. I accepted, for a few years, that antidepressants might be what I needed. Things just got worse. I had times at work when I was so exhausted that staying awake through the day became almost impossible. As a life-long planner, famous for having my life under control, I found it hard to remember what I was meant to be doing, impossible to take in new names, and excruciatingly difficult trying to maintain a positive and focused demeanour for colleagues and clients. I thought I was getting dementia. My self-confidence nose-dived.

It was pretty terrifying, and every slip-up or negative comment heightened the fear and further dented my self-esteem. Then the night sweats started. That should have lit up the menopause sign in neon brilliance. But no. Only after various blood tests for cancer, rheumatic conditions and the odd tropical disease did a second GP realize what should have been obvious for some years. Within weeks of starting hormone replacement therapy (HRT) I felt epic. I was me again, for a while at least, as hormones have a way of continuing to shape-shift as time goes on. Although life was tough, juggling family and work commitments, I no longer believed I was losing my mind to boot.

That was nine years ago and, in my case, menopause has been the gift that just keeps giving. It has been an ongoing juggling act of managing symptoms, trying to access the right medical support, and keeping the family and household going, while also endeavouring to be my best at work. I couldn't see that there would be times, like now, when things would be great again. The kids have moved on with their own exciting lives and careers giving me more space to invest in me. I have re-affirmed control of my working life by starting my own business and, despite being 'over-the-hill', last year was my most successful work year ever. And looking ahead I know I have so much more to give. With testosterone now added to my daily HRT cocktail, I have regained a long-lost focus and zest. So here I am, catching up on some of the unfinished business and frustrated ambitions I carried through my younger years, including writing this book!

Thankfully, I feel I am emerging into the light at the end of that long tunnel. However, I do look back at the challenges of the last 15 years and wonder how things might have turned out if I had understood menopause earlier and had asked for more help at work. Would my bosses have been supportive? Would they have acted, so that I could do more than simply keep my head above water? We never had that conversation and so, as is the case for many women, menopause was undoubtedly a factor in my decision to leave my job and to find another way.

I am lucky. I could use my professional skills in a way that suits me better. Other women simply quit, leaving careers that they loved. This represents a huge loss not only to them personally but also to the organizations that quietly watch them go. It's time I did my bit to address this loss.

I have worked as a business psychologist and senior executive coach for over 30 years. I have helped leaders step up and fulfil their potential, and to get the best from their teams. For women in work, this can mean addressing a different set of challenges that get in the way of their success. These challenges might be nothing about the work itself or the woman's capabilities. In fact, my earliest encounter with this was as an undergraduate at Oxford University. For my dissertation I had been learning about the models that predict stress at work. In 1990, the models all focused on stressors within work itself. To my mind, this instantly made the models less relevant and useful for working women, who I proposed would be more challenged by the interplay between work and home life. My research findings supported this, as has the research of many others since. We need to look at women's working lives through a very different lens from the one we would use for men. In my own company, Brew People, we support organizations in taking a systemic approach that recognizes the wider issues that impact people at work.

Many positive things have happened to help women progress and thrive in their careers. In spite of this, women are still a relative rarity in the most senior roles. Systemic barriers still get in the way. Women still disproportionately carry the can on the domestic front, which can put them on an alternative career path and earnings track. And women continue to experience gender bias that blocks them from the opportunities and rewards that their male colleagues receive. Increasing numbers of incredible 50-something women do manage to stay the course and break through to the most senior roles. Only now, as many tell me, they have new emerging challenges holding them back. Challenges with their health, well-being and confidence. Challenges that are distinctly different from those described by senior male leaders of a similar age and which seem inextricably linked to menopause.

Like others, my experience of the slow chaotic arrival of menopause has been a process of dealing with little-understood physical changes, but also rethinking my identity, fighting for my sense of worth and re-establishing my place in the working world. Medical intervention has helped but it hasn't completely eradicated all the symptoms and the physical, cognitive and emotional challenges that come along with these. Even if I had been able to access the best medical support earlier, life would have been so much better if I had also been able to access better support at work.

I believe more can be done in workplaces to help women sustain their performance and well-being through menopause. Things are changing rapidly with a growing availability of help and information. However, for business leaders who want to play their part, it takes a bit of work to find out how. I hope this book will make a difference and enable many more organizations to become menopause friendly via an actionable plan.

Introduction

This book is for business leaders. It is the book I wish my bosses had been able to access and which I hope will help organizations support women better in the future. Whether you are a team leader, HR business partner, senior executive or board member, this is the book I'd like you to lean into, as I cannot imagine a time when organizations will not need to engage and enable women through menopause.

The book is structured in two parts. In Part 1, I explain why menopause is an issue for working women and why employers cannot afford to be complacent about it. When symptoms and work expectations collide, it becomes difficult for women to keep participating, performing, progressing and thriving. This is costly for women but also for organizations. The business case for taking action is clear.

In Part 2, I draw on a growing well of evidence on menopause, an expert understanding of how to empower people at work and a systems-thinking approach that will help you to lead meaningful change. I propose a new framework, M-POWERED, for creating and implementing an effective menopause action plan.

Shifting attitudes and knowledge outside work

Over the last 10 years, an enormous amount has changed in the public discourse around menopause. Menopause used to be taboo, but now women can raise the topic with far greater confidence. Women in the public eye have made enormously valuable contributions towards de-stigmatizing menopause. Cool, attractive, intelligent and creative women like Mariella Frostrup and Davina McCall have publicly shared their own experiences. They have shown that it's ok to mention your drying, leaking, aching, sleepless, anxious conditions, and other women are beginning to ask, 'Why should I stay quiet?'

Away from the public eye, more women are discussing menopause with one another and their partners and families. By bringing menopause out of the shadows, they are now far better equipped to find support from doctors and health professionals, nutritionists, fitness experts, well-being practitioners and, indeed, from one another. Women are sharing with each other what they have learned and what has personally worked for them. The knowledge base available to women is, therefore, growing. This is enormously empowering. Women no longer feel they must simply endure symptoms or accept solutions that don't actually work for them. They can advocate more powerfully for themselves and assert a need for support or treatment where it is impacting their lives.

This growth of interest and dialogue is far more than just a talking-shop or something of dry academic interest. It is super-charged with urgency. It is fuelled by anger, frustration and sadness at the lack of understanding and support that women have been given historically around their own bodies. However, it is also powered by hope, generating optimism that there are things that can make a positive difference.

We know that those experiencing symptoms of menopause are far more likely to leave their careers, take a step back or say 'No thank you' to the next promotion. As a result, many organizations have taken important steps to address the taboo of menopause, to consider the impact it has on women's careers and to find ways to support women through this inevitable stage of their lives, such as through achieving 'Menopause Friendly' accreditation.[1] This is, nevertheless, new ground for all of us and there is surprisingly little that you can pick off the shelf that will guide leaders on the strategic and practical actions they can take. With the growing urgency on this subject, workplaces need to catch up.

Why it pays for organizations to take action

In many countries, women of menopausal age are the fastest-growing demographic in the workplace. Increasingly, women want and need to continue working to their full potential through menopause and beyond. However, there is a growing awareness that the symptoms of menopause can hold women back. This impact can be felt from women's early 40s, or much earlier in some cases, but the picture can be complex. Not everyone experiences menopause in the same way, and the effect of hormonal change is compounded by other external pressures that women often experience at the same time in their lives. Without the right support through menopause, many leave their careers, hold back from promotions or feel unable to be fully productive. As a result, they lose out on earnings, long-term retirement savings and personal fulfilment.

Organizations that invest in menopause-friendly strategies deliver benefits for women, but also see improved attraction, retention and talent optimization. This helps organizations to deliver their strategic goals: competing for talent, customers and adding shareholder value. However, the longer women stay economically active, the better it is for wider society too. As a result, there is likely to be increasing government pressure for employers to play their part and legal action against those who don't.

The business case for taking action on menopause is increasingly strong. However, organizations are not automatically menopause friendly. A range of systemic barriers can get in the way. This starts with the taboo that surrounds menopause. We simply have not given women and their needs at this stage of life sufficient attention and too often have found conversations about menopause uncomfortable. This means that when women are struggling, we can be at a loss of what to do and what to say.

Making your organization menopause friendly

In 2024, the UK voted in a new Labour Government that had made a manifesto commitment to take action on menopause in work. This builds on work of the previous Conservative Government that had appointed a Menopause Champion to further drive change and to coordinate the sharing of learning. Expected changes to employment law could mean large employers are required to publish a menopause action plan and communicate policies to staff.[2] However, even without a change in the law, there is already a push for employers to take action.

Part 2 of this book offers the M-POWERED framework for delivering an action plan. It incorporates advice from the UK Government, the UK's Advisory, Conciliation and Arbitration Service (ACAS), and the Chartered Institute of Personnel and Development (CIPD). It is also supported by research and insight from work psychology and best practice organizational case studies.

Brew People's M-POWERED framework

Empowerment is at the heart of Brew People's framework. As women experience menopause, the onset of difficult symptoms alongside challenging work and home demands can fundamentally impact a woman's sense of clarity, confidence, control and connection – in other words, the fundamentals of empowerment. If organizations do not take action to be more menopause friendly, they can significantly worsen the impact.

Enabling greater empowerment for women working through menopause means delivering systemic change. The best action plan must incorporate all these elements:

Purpose	Ensuring the whole organization is committed to empowering women.
Openness	Breaking taboo so that women can voice their needs and secure support.
Will	Offering women flexibility and choice in how they can best perform.
Effectiveness	Helping women realize their strengths and potential.
Relationships	Building a menopause-friendly community to counter feelings of isolation.
Environment	Designing work environments adapted to women's needs.
Delivery	Planning for sustained systemic measurable change.

Brew People's new M-POWERED framework is introduced in Part 2, the remainder of the book translating the framework into practical actions.

It's complicated!

There are various challenges in writing about menopause. Where possible I have tried to find the right balance between some alternative objectives and perspectives. I hope the book is sufficiently simple that you will get what you need from it and feel confident to move forward with an action plan. However, I also hope that I have given a respectful nod to the complexities that lie behind the headline messages and the action planning guidelines. As a starting point, it may be helpful to clarify some of the terminology I use in the book. While this can be perceived as straightforward, it can sometimes mask a more complex picture beneath.

Menopause as a process

First, let me address the use of the term 'menopause'. In medical terms, menopause is a point of time 12 months after someone's last period. However, I generally adopt the everyday usage of 'menopause' to describe the whole process from perimenopause through to post-menopause. The process has unique impacts for each woman, so I often refer to someone's 'menopause experience' to highlight its personal nature. I also, at times, refer to the 'menopause transition' to underline that menopause is a period of change that often resolves positively.

Menopause seen through a biopsychosocial lens

Principally, we think of menopause as something that happens to women's bodies. In turn, we observe that physical symptoms can trigger challenges with a woman's psychological state and how she interacts with the world.

There is, in fact, evidence that the symptoms experienced can also be influenced in reverse, by a woman's psychological strategies, her cultural environment and her personal experiences.[3] Throughout the book, I underline these multi-directional influences impacting menopause, adopting a 'biopsychosocial' approach. Recognizing the impact of mindset on symptoms is not to suggest that a woman is to blame if she encounters greater difficulties. However, it aims to address the true complexity of each individuals' experience and the potential to improve outcomes by addressing menopause concurrently from these three different angles: medical, psychological and environmental.

Women as a key focus

A key simplification in the book is my reference throughout to 'women'. This is representative of most people who experience menopause. The experience of menopause is also intertwined with other factors that women are more likely to experience. However, it should be remembered that menopause can be experienced by trans and non-binary people. Indeed, the impact of menopause can be uniquely challenging for those who would not see themselves as women. This community also needs sensitivity and support, and I hope the book, at least partly, answers to that need.

Why I talk about 'older women'

Menopause can be experienced by younger women in their 20s, 30s or early 40s. However, I regularly refer to 'older women', as perimenopause and menopause is typically associated with ageing and experienced by those who are middle-aged or in their later years. Many who fall in the 45-plus age brackets will not see themselves as 'old' or 'older'. However, they may begin to experience the health impacts of ageing and, concurrently, sense a shift in how they are perceived by others and their own sense of self.

Menopause as a global issue

The book presents menopause as an issue impacting organizations globally but also touches on the need to consider national, cultural and ethnic differences. However, this is a new developing field, and global research can be hard to source. Several writers and commentators have noted that the UK is pushing ahead with research and policies addressing menopause at work, and this can mean that the book reflects a more UK-centric perspective.

PART 1
THE CASE FOR TAKING ACTION

1
Time for a re-think on menopause

If we step back, we can see that work has always evolved in response to wider societal change. And, as work changes, so does its relationship to women change. Even so, the way organizations have developed has not always made it easy for women to participate to their full potential. As we move forward, we see organizations are continuing to re-think how they are designed so that they better capitalize on women's talents, resilience and industriousness through their whole career. Attention is now focusing on how this is achieved for women's later careers as they experience the menopause transition.

In this chapter, I explore the impact of an ageing workforce and the unique challenges that menopause can precipitate for women during their middle and later careers. Older women represent the fastest growing demographic in the workforce, and with every one of them going through menopause at some point, there is evidence of women suffering a menopause penalty in their earnings and progression. While menopause can be experienced by younger women, I highlight the interplay between menopausal health issues and concurrent life experiences for women in their mid-40s and older. Finally, I point to the importance of organizations taking action, and the benefits this can deliver for women, organizations, and society as a whole.

What's new about old women?

Menopause is an inevitable stage that usually accompanies natural ageing, although for some can occur suddenly or prematurely (see Chapter 2). We might ask whether it deserves special attention over and above the impact that ageing can have for both men and women. Certainly, we should look at menopause within the context of a broadly shifting demographic at work but there is good reason to prioritize older women within people strategies. In this section I outline how men and women are differentially impacted by ageing. I also outline how, despite the challenges many women experience with their health, their numbers at work are increasing at a faster rate than any other demographic group. While the rate of growth in this cohort will settle in time, older women will continue to represent a significant proportion of an organization's total workforce. No organization can afford to ignore the issue of menopause.

Our ageing workforce

The face of the average worker is not what it was 50 years ago. Our life expectancy today dwarfs that of previous generations. Added to this we see falling birth rates. Organizations must plan for a changing demographic balance with a lot more grey hairs and wrinkles on display. The CIPD reported in 2021,[4] that nearly one-third of workers in the UK were aged 50 and over (32.6%). This had increased by 50% (from 21%) in the 1990s. In fact, figures could be even higher, as UK national data only collates worker numbers up to the age of 64 reflecting, now outdated, statutory retirement ages. Not even our statistical systems can keep up with the pace of change!

The Covid pandemic significantly dented this trajectory with fewer older workers in 2023 than there had been in 2019. During Covid, older workers found themselves more likely to be made redundant and less likely to gain new employment as a result of age discrimination.[5] They were also more likely to leave due to ill-health in this period, with a significant increase in those unable to return due to long-term sickness. Nevertheless, the increase in older workers is reflective of a longer-term trend that mirrors the increasingly ageing population in the UK.

Many older people need to and want to work. Pension ages keep rising and long leisurely retirements are not for everyone. Many older workers still enjoy their work, want to pursue new challenges and want to (or have to) keep earning. Organizations, meanwhile, need older people to stay. This might require investment in training and development so that older talent keeps pace with change. Even so, it's vital that organizations retain valuable experience, expertise and organizational wisdom, and, if nothing else, headcount. They know that the demographic shift means a shrinking pool of younger talent to draw from and that older workers cannot be easily replaced.

Sadly, the increase in life expectancy does not equate to an increase in healthy-life expectancy. Both men and women can be affected by health issues as they grow older, which, in turn, can affect their work. To make work sustainable in older age, organizations must consider how they will handle potential health issues in the older workforce. Below the age of 40, the number of workers limited by health issues is relatively consistent at around 10–12%, but this steeply increases beyond the age of 40. CIPD research showed that one in four workers in the UK reaches a point, before retirement, at which their work is limited by a health condition.[6] Ill health is the main reason for giving up a job for the over 50s, especially in the poorest households where health levels are lower and where the work carried out is often more physically demanding.[7]

Poor health impacts both the kind of work people can do and the amount of work they can do. Increasing numbers of people address this by taking up flexible working opportunities, choosing both where they work and the hours they work, or by shifting to self-employment. However, not everyone has access to these options, which leads to increasing levels of economic inactivity for older people ahead of their official retirement age.

Turning our attention to women, we can see that health issues related to ageing are a particular challenge, with menopause triggering an earlier decline in health. At the time of the industrial revolution women, typically, would not have lived to more than 50 years of age; so menopause was a very brief moment coinciding with the end stage of life. In 2020, UK women lived on average to around 83 years of age. OECD 2022 and 2023 figures show that, globally, women outlive men by around five years. Unfortunately, they are likely to spend a far greater proportion of their later life in ill health as health appears to decline from an earlier age than men. This has obvious knock-on effects for women's participation in work.[8]

Alongside increased life expectancy, retirement ages between men and women are converging with women seeing the most rapid increase. In the UK, women born in 1950 were expected to retire at 60, while those born only 11 years later in 1961 have seen retirement ages reach 67 years.[9] These are drastic changes in a short space of time with the consequence that menopause now impacts up to a half of a woman's life, and maybe one-third of her working life. Unfortunately, women reaching menopausal age could find that the last 20 years of their careers are spent dealing with an array of health issues stemming from menopause. This is markedly different from men who, typically, do not experience such a clear and early tipping point in their health.

The rise of older women at work

Despite the differential impact of health and ageing, the number of women in work is rising. Within the UK, census data shows that women's rates of employment are catching up with men's: around 72% in 2023 (from around 62% in the early 1990s).[10] This compares to a male employment rate of 78%, which has remained fairly steady over the same time period. Growth in female participation is seen worldwide with the OECD recording the gender employment gap closing to only 11% in 2022, from 18% in 2000.[11] However, it is particularly interesting that the largest increases for women are seen in the older age groups. By 2025, globally, over 555 billion working women will be over the age of 45.[12] In the US, more than half of workers are now women, and 45% of these women are over 45 and potentially approaching or past menopause.[13] If you add in those who may be experiencing menopause earlier, then you could say that currently around a quarter of all workers in the US are personally impacted by menopause.

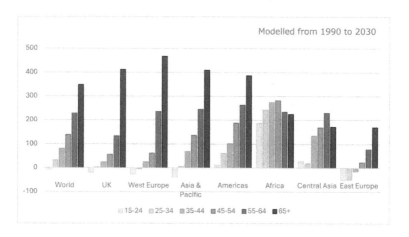

Figure 1.1: *Percentage change of women who are economically active by age group and region.*

Source: https://ourworldindata.org/grapher/female-labor-force-by-age (ILOSTAT ILO modelled estimates: Labour force by sex and age – ILO modelled estimates, July 2017 (thousands) – 10-year age bands: 15-24 - Sex: Female – processed by Our World in Data).

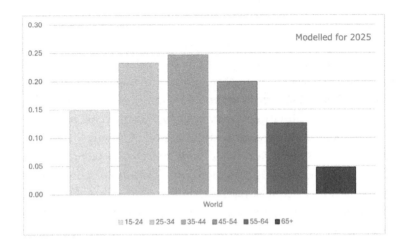

Figure 1.2: Percentage of total women who are economically active by age group, worldwide.

Source: https://ourworldindata.org/grapher/female-labor-force-by-age (ILOSTAT ILO modelled estimates: Labour force by sex and age – ILO modelled estimates, July 2017 (thousands) – 10-year age bands: 15–24 – Sex: Female – processed by Our World in Data).

The current generation of menopausal women are a new phenomenon for employers. Three generations ago, in many respects women were considered too delicate and unmanageable to hold down professions at all,[14] unless they belonged to the social underclass in which case they often carried out poorly rewarded hard graft. Two generations ago in the 1940s, women may have worked for a while but were expected to give up work when they married, dedicating their energy to raising a family and keeping the home.[15] A generation after that, in the 1970s women often married later or stayed in work beyond marriage. They chose to have fewer children or have them later on, but then usually gave up work or were forced to leave once children arrived. From the 1970s things changed again with the introduction of stronger women's employment rights. This enabled many more women to carry on working alongside parenting. They faced the possibility of sustaining both a fulfilling career and also a life of domestic bliss.

The present day: Increasing numbers working into older age, with children still at home, or whilst grandparenting.

1970s onwards: Most women worked through motherhood. Increased numbers delaying parenthood.

1950s–1970s: Women worked after marriage until start of motherhood.

1900–1950s: Women usually worked until married.

Pre 1900s: Women often educated but with limited opportunities for work.

Figure 1.3: Russian dolls representing women's changing participation in paid work.

Of course, the reality for Gen X women has been a never-ending juggling act of overwork and compromise. But many women have succeeded in having at least some parts of 'it all'. They have made important contributions to wider society and within paid employment while also being wives and mothers. Only now, this same cohort of women whom we encouraged to step forward into the working world are the very ones boosting the figures of 50-something women who are working today. They bring with them a set of health and social issues not seen in any generation of working women before them. Yet they are still passionate about their careers, resilient from a lifetime of breaking boundaries, and still full of potential to keep growing and contributing.

Why women keep on working

There are many factors that might motivate today's older women to keep a career going beyond menopause despite increasing health issues. For many they simply 'have to'. Employers may still convey an attitude that a woman's career is an optional luxury within a household. However, Palermo et al. demonstrated that financial security is a significant factor in keeping women in work.[16] Among older women, those who work are more likely to be single, struggling financially, have financial dependents or not own their own homes. With pension ages set to keep rising, and with years of part-time working and maternity breaks behind them, they have a much smaller pension pot to fall back on than their ageing male counterparts and are mindful of the need to catch up.[17]

That doesn't mean that all women are eyeing the door for their first chance of an exit. The reality is that women often want to work – not just for the money but also for personal fulfilment. They want to participate and to contribute. They want to develop and sustain their professional identity. They want to use their brains and talents. Although the pressure to keep earning can be acute, the IFS show that the fastest rate of growth in working women has been among those who already have a high-earning partner.[18] This suggests the driver is one of fulfilling potential rather than necessity.

When women don't feel fulfilled, the more financially secure will be the first to question the value of battling on. However, Palermo's study showed that while economic factors might keep an older woman in work, the rate at which people leave is highest where women don't feel appreciated, able to physically cope, feel less satisfied with the work itself or where they lack control due to being employed rather than self-employed.

Evidence of a menopause penalty

Regardless of how much women want to or need to work, the evidence is clear. A barrier exists for menopausal women shown through the widening gender pay gap in later careers. We know that both men and women see their earning potential start to wane as they move into older age and that this can happen long before retirement due to the onset of physical and mental changes and due to age discrimination. Earnings tend to peak in both men and women in their 40s.[19] However, there appears to be a cliff edge in earning differentials that emerges at this point.[20] While men's earning peak at 47 years of age, women's peak a full five years earlier at 42. From this point onwards the gender pay gap widens, demonstrating a divergence in women's and men's earning potential in their run up to retirement. In 2023, the UK gender pay gap at 40–49 was 10.3%, whereas at age 30–39 it was relatively low at 4.7% (2.3% in 2022).

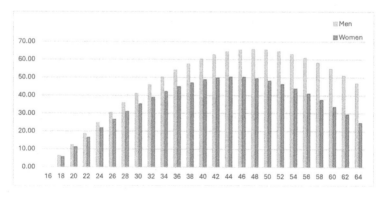

Figure 1.4: Percentage growth in mean hourly pay by gender for full-time employees in private sector, 2017.

Source: *Office for National Statistics licensed under the Open Government Licence v.3.0 (Office for National Statistics. (2018). Employee earnings in the UK: 2018).*

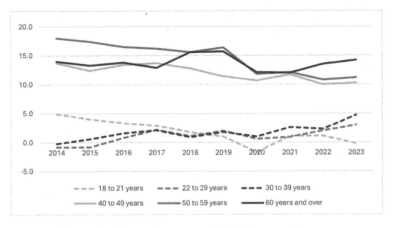

Figure 1.5: UK gender pay gap for full time median gross hourly earnings by age group.

Source: Adapted from data from the Office for National Statistics licensed under the Open Government Licence v. 1.0 (Office for National Statistics (2023), Gender pay gap in the UK: 2023).

A gender pay gap emerges early in women's careers. The OECD put 40% of this down to discrimination and 60% to the motherhood penalty[21] (where careers are disrupted by maternity leave and childcare pressures). It has been recognized that over time this early gap becomes compounded. Now there is a growing recognition that menopause is a significant driver that exacerbates the gender pay gap. An IFS study in Norway and Sweden outlined the evidence for a menopause 'penalty' in earnings that represents an earning loss of around 20% relative to pre-menopause levels.[22] We know that health is a key reason why people, in general, shift towards part-time working. We also know that older women are far more likely than men to take up the option of part-time work, and a lower pay packet, as their health worsens earlier[23] and due to the multiple demands they face outside of work. We also know that the most senior and well-paid roles are less likely to be offered on anything other than a full-time basis, further curtailing the potential of women to fully utilize their talents. In the meantime, as men age, they are more likely to move into more inflexible 'greedy' jobs that reward presenteeism and over-work, serving to further widen the gender pay gap.[24]

Unfortunately, many women begin to suffer financial hardship in their middle years. The impact of caring responsibilities,[25] plus divorce,[26] plus menopause[27] all build up the pressure on women's finances. As a result of menopause, it becomes increasingly difficult to fill the hole left in women's savings. In 2020, the UK government published data showing a 35% pension pay gap for women relative to men by the age of 55 years. The gap is made worse through divorce where women's pension wealth is more significantly reduced as a result.[28]

Menopausal women have a lot going on

If menopause itself isn't enough to deal with, very often it occurs when women are contending with a whole host of other challenges. What's more, it is often these additional pressures that make it difficult for women to have their health challenges taken seriously, as symptoms are often put down to stress alone. Whether or not menopause has become a condition requiring medical support, it certainly can be wrapped up in a complex web of issues for women at this time of their lives. It is important to appreciate this wider picture to fully understand what working women may be dealing with.

Figure 1.6: Many women juggle a range of responsibilities and pressures alongside the effects of menopause.

The moonlight sonata

Women are, in effect, professional moonlighters. Regardless of how committed they are to their careers, they still do more of the unpaid work at home than their male partners, effectively juggling two separate jobs. The UK Office for National Statistics found that in a sample period in 2023, women spent over 3.5 hours per day doing unpaid work activities such as housework, caring for others and volunteering. That's nearly an hour more, per day, than men.[29] Many working women might make space for unpaid work by opting for part-time employment. However, even full-time working women are likely to do more than their fair share at home. A study by the Pew Research Center in the United States of America found that even where women are equal breadwinners, they still do 4.5 hours more housework and caregiving than their male partners, who can spend 3.5 hours more on leisure activities.[30]

While women may want to focus on their career development and earnings, and may have the support of their employers to do so, the pressure to keep homes, families and community interests going can be an additional bar to women's participation, performance, progression and well-being. It has been shown that the additional burden of unpaid work takes its toll on women's mental health regardless of whether menopause is also presenting a challenge.[31] For women who are menopausal and struggling with joint and muscle pain or sleeplessness, the physicality of household chores can be hard to sustain. Brain fog, another common symptom, can affect concentration, planning and memory. Yet women can feel an excessive burden to plan and manage the home and family making such cognitive symptoms additionally difficult. Meanwhile, the time and headspace given to household responsibilities can make it very difficult for women to schedule exercise and prioritize healthy eating, both of which can be hugely helpful during menopause.

All hail the sandwich generation!

Many Gen X women elected to delay having kids while studying and establishing careers. Having children later on, has meant a significant shift in how generations overlap and how parenting intersects with other aspects of life. It is not uncommon for women to have teenagers at home with all the pressures and hormonal angst that this can entail, while also being hit with a hormonal maelstrom of their own, providing a double shot of emotional strain. In fact, in 2021, the average age in the UK for a mother giving birth was 30.9 years, meaning it would be highly likely that perimenopause would be experienced while a child was still at home.[32] Indeed, for women who give birth in their mid- to late 30s, the signs of perimenopause may already be kicking in while caring for a newborn baby. Chronic sleeplessness is likely to result in knock-on consequences for physical and mental health.

Changes in generational overlaps mean today's menopausal women don't usually fit the archetypal grandmother image. Rather, they are more likely to be sandwiched between children and their older parents. Older parents may be active and healthy and a source of great support to women (special thanks to my mum who was an amazing powerhouse of support for me through this time). However, very often working mothers will find themselves concurrently providing practical and emotional support to their children *and* their parents. Age UK reports that there are 1.25 million such sandwich carers in the UK, 68% of whom are women. Sandwich carers can range in age from their 20s to 60s but are most likely to fall in the 35–44 year old age range,[33] when many will be experiencing the first signs and symptoms of perimenopause.

So long, farewell…

The picture painted in previous paragraphs is one of women taking on more and more. At the same time the years around menopause can also represent a time of profound loss. While dealing with the symptoms of menopause, women might have the additional challenge of trying to re-define who they are in the face of huge change.

As women enter their 50s, they are likely to start, or finish, waving goodbye to the young adults they have nurtured and raised. Though an increasing number of kids 'boomerang' back home for a time, there can be a huge adjustment to the gradually emptying nest. It can be a time of wonderful opportunity for women to re-invent themselves, and perhaps reconnect with their younger selves. It may also be a time when women can start to throw energies back into careers. However, before embracing any potential newfound direction and identity, women can live through a period of heartbreak and letting go of the old.[34] This time can be a period of great emotional instability where women re-consider what their purpose is and what they really want for themselves.

Midlife is a challenging time for everyone. With the pressures of work, family finances and children, many marriages do not survive the strain. Divorce rates are highest between the ages of 35 and 55 but peak in people's mid-40s.[35] This often leaves women raising children as single parents. The rate of lone-parent households in the UK is much higher than in other European countries (23% versus 13%), although the rate has stayed fairly consistent over the last 20 years. One-third (33%) will, at some point, have been a lone-parent family, and around 90% of such households are headed up by women. Single-parent households are associated with far greater family stress and poverty, while concurrently making it harder for the single parent to sustain work.[36] Divorced women may be struggling with the loss of household support, financial security and social identity while also tackling newfound health issues.

The changing world for working women

As the relationship between women and work evolves, we continue to see a shifting balance between the interests and motivations of workers, their employers and national interests pursued by government. There is good evidence that organizations are not as menopause friendly as they could be, with menopause being a key driver of inequity. However, today we see a growing desire from women, employers and society at large to ensure work is more inclusive for older women.

The evolution of work and its impact for women

When we look back over time, we see how external change has always played its part in determining how organizations operate. This has resulted in a changing relationship between women and the world of work.

In the ancient world, work was simply that which required effort or skill or which 'got stuff done'. There was little distinction between work at home or work beyond the home, and everyone had to do their bit; men, women and children all laboured to get food on the table. Right up to the Industrial Revolution, up to 90% of people, the world over, worked in agriculture.[37] For these people, work–life balance was non-existent, as life was all about work. Those who didn't work on the fields might adopt a skilled craft or trade, producing goods that could be sold or exchanged. Although men might guard access to some of the more lucrative or illustrious crafts, women nevertheless had access to a wide variety of roles, with specialized work often being carried out from home. Working from home meant that work could be completed while at the same time keeping an eye on children and tending to the household. Therefore, through this period, although women may have taken more responsibility for domestic chores, there was less utility in differentiating between men's work and women's work with people working more as a connected community.

The biggest changes in how we work, and in women's relationship to paid employment, started within Britain in the 18th century[38] when home and work became separated. This period saw the invention of technology such as steam power, the manufacture of steel, and mechanized production of cloth. It also saw the birth of the first dedicated office buildings, created to house the vast administrative management of the British Empire.[39] Having specialized equipment and buildings meant the focus moved from the work of individual artisans at home towards getting stuff done on a large scale on-site. Business owners chased after efficiencies and competed with one another by trying to maximize productivity while minimizing wage costs. Men, women and children gave up on subsistence farming and accepted wages in return for labour, with work fast becoming short-hand for paid employment. Those who could not dedicate their time to attending a factory for long uninterrupted hours, perhaps with infants at home to care for, would become excluded from this new way of working. And so began a pattern that has largely continued until today.

The new industrialized way of working brought with it significant social advancements but also significant social costs. Workers may have been freed from the uncertainties and hardships of working the land, but often found themselves at the mercy of employers, forced to accept poor conditions and pay or face having no work at all. In many ways, life became worse for the working classes. And so, with the health and fertility of the country at stake, the government was forced to intervene, introducing the first ever labour laws designed to protect worker's rights. Laws were introduced within the UK that restricted the work demands on children and women, and which required the maintenance of sanitary and safe conditions.[40] Work was no longer simply a contractual agreement between employer and employee but also had to balance the influence of regulatory powers put in place to deliver wider societal benefit.

For over a century, women more typically stayed at home carrying out essential but unpaid domestic labour, while men and older children went out for wages. However, over time we lost sight of women's diverse potential. Women remained largely absent in workplaces. Those who did carry out paid work often took on production roles with low wages and at a cost to their health and well-being. It suited society to have women carry the domestic load, so the highest-paid jobs became the preserve of men. As a consequence, society started to believe that women shouldn't work. Furthermore, rather than seeing women's absence from workplaces as an unfortunate artefact of Victorian work design, society began to think that women lacked ability and, therefore, couldn't work. The long-term exclusion of women from workplaces contributed to a lack of belief in women's potential.

There were times when societal upheaval challenged this view and shed light on what women's contribution could be. For example, in the First and Second World Wars, with so many men away, women were needed in munition factories, on the buses and railways, and in the police – all places previously reserved for male employees. Women also played critical roles on the front lines of conflict themselves. Organizations were unable to function without women, and the country's war effort would have faltered without the additional skilled labour. Women themselves wanted to contribute and play an equal role in society. They had been campaigning for the right to vote and were more than ready to step into more physical and intellectually challenging roles than had been possible before. Everything was aligned to trigger a change.

After the First World War women were barred again from male occupations as the government saw greater value in prioritizing men's paid employment. However, many women did carry on working. They needed to. The war meant that many were left with little prospect of marriage and could not depend financially on boyfriends or husbands who never returned.

Around 9% of British men under the age of 45 were lost in the First World War,[41] with a large proportion in what would have been considered the social and educational elite. This left more women needing to be financially independent and with critical gaps in organizations to be filled. Yet again, women's relationship with work shifted in response to their own changing needs, the interests of business, the context of demographic change and the influence of government.

How women's relationship with work continues to change

As we move into the 2020s, we witness further significant pressures for change in a world facing economic and political turmoil, where the participation of women at work has become even more critical for employers. The COVID-19 pandemic taught us that rapid, radical change is possible, and this can create opportunities for improving female inclusion. As a consequence, organizations continue to experiment with remote or hybrid working, and with greater flexibility regarding working hours – the movement to trial a four-day week (where employees are paid the same wages while working fewer days) acting as a testament to this new creative urge.[42]

Any change can bring advantages but at the same time introduce new challenges. Working through lockdowns brought into focus how change can differentially impact men and women.[43] Many women, who had previously been denied the chance, were allowed to prove that they really could get their job done from home and be more (rather than less) productive.[44] However, during lockdowns women also experienced disproportionate pressures from home-schooling or shielding elderly parents, resulting in far higher role conflict and psychological distress. Women tended to take on more of these duties whether working or not, while men only took on extra caring duties if unemployed or furloughed.[45] For many women, this additional conflict triggered a desire to step further away from work roles.

Men, on the other hand, had potentially more to lose than gain through home working. Historically, men had always been in the office. They were consistently seen to be 'at work'. Proximity bias rewarded them with greater perceived commitment and capability and, consequently, greater work opportunity.[46] This advantage may have faltered during the pandemic. However, during lockdowns, men often found other ways to benefit. They were able to invest the time saved from commuting in professional development. For academics this translated into a disproportionate increase in paper submissions from men during this period[47] adding to male academics' future earning potential.

Looking to the future, the question is not 'if' an organization should change in response to menopause but one of 'how' it should change. The shifting sands of economics, politics and social life all create volatility and can trigger a re-think. What worked before, enabling an organization to compete or to deliver greatest impact, doesn't necessarily work forever. Over time work naturally evolves, bringing with it changes in who works, where they work and how they work. A sudden or long-term shift in the environment or market within which an organization operates might demand a re-think of how to engage people and technology and processes.

The multiple drivers of change

Successful organizations will be those that are more agile and able to flex in response to the changing context within which they operate. This means understanding and anticipating the emerging forces that will impact organizational success. A key part of this is the recognition that change for women working through menopause is both essential and inevitable. As we look ahead, there are multiple sources of pressure for change.

Pressure from women

From women's point of view, there continues to be an appetite for greater inclusion and participation within the working world. Too many women continue to suffer intellectually, emotionally and financially through being excluded from opportunity at work. Too often women are still expected to shoulder the burden of competing pressures between home and work. Increasingly, they are demanding greater support in finding a balance. When it comes to menopause, women are finding their voice and creating a swell of interest and expectation for employers and society to do more.

Pressure from government

From a societal point of view, it is understood that everyone benefits when women stay in work. National economic growth suffers unless women can access work opportunities.[48] The prosperity of families, particularly of single mothers, is negatively impacted unless women can continue to fulfil their earning potential. However, the health and well-being of women and, in turn, their families is diminished if organizations do not adequately support women's ability to balance work with family life. This means governments are bound to intervene and establish guiderails for maintaining female participation, including through menopause.

Pressure from employers

From an organizational point of view, there is a growing recognition that it is costly to miss out on the contributions of talented and motivated older workers, including older women. Without this valuable commodity organizations will struggle to grow and compete. There is also a recognition that this cannot be achieved without change. An 'all or nothing' approach to staffing that assumes a full-time commitment with zero impact from health issues or family commitments is simply unrealistic. Employers must respond to women's changing expectations. They must also ready themselves for the changing demands from government.

It's clear that it is time for a re-think on menopause. How we work is always evolving, but rapid demographic changes reveal a need to focus right now on older women in the workplace. This fast-growing cohort need to and want to work but experience a range of concurrent challenges. Everyone will benefit if these challenges are better addressed.

Key themes in Chapter 1

1. Employers need to attract, retain and develop older workers.
2. Health is an issue for older workers, but menopause can trigger health issues earlier for women, demanding extra attention.
3. Menopause can coincide with other pressures in women's lives.
4. The number of older women in work, who may be impacted by menopause, is growing significantly.
5. A menopause penalty contributes to the gender pay gap.
6. Understanding the evolution of women's relationship with work can help us to shape future change.
7. Pressure for change comes from women, government, and employers themselves.

2
Understanding the menopause transition and its impact

Menopause is a natural process, albeit one that can have debilitating effects for both the body and mind. The experience of menopause and the run up to it is hugely varied. In the past we tended to think of menopause symptoms as only involving hot flushes (flashes in the United States). Now we recognize a wide range of physical, emotional and cognitive symptoms that accompany menopause. Rather than just suffering in silence, women are becoming more empowered to find strategies for managing their menopause symptoms. Medical solutions can offer a lifeline for many. Even so, women very often find their symptoms have a negative impact on their work. As a result, many women find it unsustainable to carry on with full time work, or in some cases to continue with paid employment at all. Those who do soldier on often see their performance suffer and can lose confidence, holding back from further opportunities for challenge and growth.

In this chapter, I offer insight in the hormone changes both women and men experience and the form this can take when women experience menopause. I highlight the wide range of possible symptoms and the opportunities and challenges in managing these. I finally explore the consequences for women at work.

All aboard the hormone roller-coaster

From 2010 to 2025, our understanding of menopause has changed dramatically. We have gone from seeing menopause simply as the end of fertility marked by embarrassing hot flushes and leaky bladders to recognizing multiple complex effects on women's bodies and minds.

It is helpful to view menopause in the context of wider hormonal systems in the body and the impact these have for long-term health. Both men's and women's bodies are in a constant state of hormonal flux throughout their lives but there are times when things can get more seriously out of balance. The symptoms of hormone deficiency and change can be experienced by anyone, sometimes triggered by other health issues, medical treatments or elective hormone therapy. However, something distinctive happens for women as they transition through menopause. Hormone levels can become erratic for years before levelling out with significant variation in individual experience.

A life in constant balance

All of us are becoming more familiar with a range of hormones that are essential for how our body functions – for example, insulin for our metabolism and adrenaline for how we respond to stress. Hormones work in concert as a complex chemical soup, washing around our bodies in a constant ebb and flow. Our bodies are not in a single fixed state but continually adjusting a wide range of hormone levels to optimize how we respond to external and internal conditions.

We may not always succeed in achieving and maintaining the optimum levels we need as we adapt to changing conditions. As a result of issues with diet, sleep, fitness, genetics, ageing and damage from disease, we know that hormonal systems can go wrong. For example, long-term stress can have a destabilizing impact on our metabolism. High levels of cortisol and adrenaline, the hormones triggered by stress, stimulate the body to metabolize fat and carbohydrates faster. This prepares the body for a flight, fight or freeze response. However, it also triggers an increased appetite and can drive people towards eating higher-energy foods, impacting our brain and behaviour. If this becomes a sustained pattern over time, it can contribute to insulin resistance and type 2 diabetes, heightening the risk of diabetes complications.[49]

For women, the complexity of their endocrine system is increased by the tidal patterns of the sex hormones driving the menstrual cycle. This complexity has long been used as a reason for excluding women from medical research[50] leading to gaps in our understanding. For example, polycystic ovary syndrome (PCOS) is a relatively common condition impacting around 1 in 10 women of childbearing age. It is thought to involve interactions between testosterone and insulin. Symptoms can be serious, affecting the metabolism, cardiovascular health and fertility, but due to limited research it remains poorly understood.[51] Meanwhile, menopause impacts every woman but it is clear that even on this we are still learning.

More than making babies

As we have learned in recent years, sex hormones have a complexity and impact that goes far beyond reproduction. It turns out that all of us have hormones we had been led to think were exclusively male or female. Research in this area is still developing but there are strong indications that sex hormones are critical for our overall health. It is not surprising that women experience an impact on their overall health and well-being when their sex hormones decline.

Oestrogen as a male hormone

Oestrogen has long been considered a female sex hormone. In females it is produced by the ovaries, and plays a significant role in female reproductive cycles and in triggering sex changes in puberty such as the development of breast tissue.[52] Higher levels of oestrogen in both women and men will trigger more feminized bodies. However, the role of oestrogen is much broader than driving physical sex differentiation. Both men and women rely on oestrogen for the healthy maintenance of muscle, bones, nervous system, skin and metabolism.

In men, oestrogen is produced mainly within the testes and plays an important positive role in male fertility. So yes, oestrogen is a female sex hormone, but it is also a male sex hormone; additionally, it is a general multi-functional health hormone – basically, it is important for everyone.[53,54]

Testosterone as a female hormone

Similarly, testosterone has long been considered a male sex hormone, as in men it is produced within the testes. Higher levels of testosterone can trigger the body to become more masculinized with a higher muscle mass, more body hair and a deeper voice. However, as with oestrogen, testosterone plays an important role beyond sexual differentiation. In both men and women, it supports bone health, insulin release and brain function.[55]

In females, testosterone is produced in the ovaries and may play a key role in some processes within the ovary and uterus. Although women typically produce seven to eight times less testosterone than men, through most of the menstrual cycle they have more testosterone in their system than oestrogen.[56]

Riding the 'big dipper'

In women, at some point, levels of oestrogen, progesterone and testosterone naturally begin to fall. This may happen gradually over several years feeling like a gentle steady decline. However, more often it is a roller-coaster of changing symptoms or, occasionally, a sudden dramatic free-fall. Because of the wide variability in experience, there is no 'normal' menopause as such. The journey is different for everyone but can be summarized in three stages: perimenopause, menopause and post-menopause. For men, the decline of sex hormones is usually steadier and more predictable as they age with far fewer obvious symptoms as a result.

Perimenopause

This can start at very different ages from a woman's mid-30s to her mid-50s, with the average being 47. It may last only a matter of months for some, or 10 years or more for others, with the average around three to four years.

In perimenopause, hormone levels start to fluctuate and ultimately reduce. Hormonal turbulence and deficiency can trigger a wide range of debilitating symptoms, which differ from person to person. Rather than being a steady predictable process it can be somewhat chaotic. Symptoms can vary day to day. Symptoms can be brought under control with support and treatment for a few years and then suddenly worsen again as the woman's body continues to change.

Menopause

Menopause is, strictly speaking, a single moment in time. When oestrogen has decreased to the point where the woman no longer has a period, and this has been the case for a full 12 months, the woman is defined as reaching menopause.

Menopause is typically reached between the ages of 45 and 55. However, between 1 in 10, and 1 in 20, will experience early menopause before the age of 45 years,[57] and 1 in 20 after the age of 55. Some may not reach menopause until over 60 years.

Distinct differences occur across cultures, ethnicities and socioeconomic conditions.[58] For example, women in the UK who are of African Caribbean origin experience an earlier menopause (average 49.7 years), with a longer perimenopause. When we look further afield, in India, women have an average menopause age of 46.7. This is much lower than the 51 years reported as the average in Western countries.[59]

Post-menopause

Beyond the 12 months in which a woman has not had a period, she is defined as post-menopausal. Within this stage, many symptoms that were problematic during perimenopause can diminish. In fact, research has shown how well-being and life satisfaction typically resurge in the post-menopause years.[60]

However, some symptoms such as hot flushes can continue for several years: 6.5% women continue to have hot flushes through to age 65.[61] Meanwhile, genito-urinary symptoms such as vulval pain, vaginal dryness, UTIs and bladder control can continue to worsen and impact quality of life.

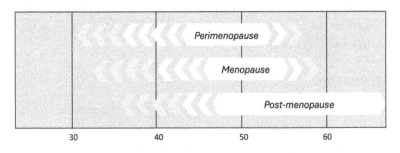

Figure 2.1a: Varying ages that women experience the key stages of menopause.

Understanding the menopause transition and its impact | 31

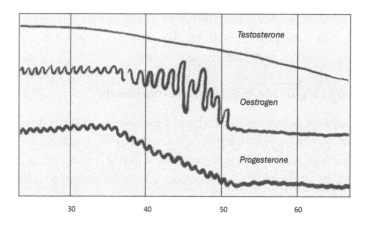

Figure 2.1b: Typical patterns of decline for testosterone, oestrogen and progesterone (does not represent actual levels of each hormone).

Sources: www.tandfonline.com/doi/full/10.2147/IJWH.S340491#d1e1357; www.frontiersin.org/journals/physiology/articles/10.3389/fphys.2018.01834/full; www.researchgate.net/publication/235400521_Testosterone_therapy_in_women_Myths_and_misconceptions#pf2

Sudden or early menopause

Understanding the typical stages of menopause can help women navigate the changes. However, there are risks in oversimplifying the path that menopause takes. There are many women who vary significantly from the norm.

▶ Menopause may start suddenly or prematurely as the result of gynaecological surgery or cancer treatment. This can plunge a woman instantly into menopause without the more usual gradual build-up. A rapid crash in hormone levels can be particularly difficult for women to experience.

▶ Menopause can occur early due to genetic variations. One in a hundred women will experience premature menopause, before the age of 40, with one in a thousand under the age of 30. Aside from the impact of lost fertility, the earlier women reach menopause the greater the long-term probability of a range of conditions such as osteoporosis and cardiovascular diseases,[62] both of which can reduce life expectancy.

Menopause in the transgender community

Menopause is not only experienced by women. A trans or non-binary person may still have a uterus and ovaries, and therefore experience menopausal symptoms while presenting to the world as a man. In fact, menopause may be triggered earlier for some trans men if receiving testosterone therapy.[63] A trans woman, on the other hand, may be receiving gender-affirming hormone therapy and, as a result, experience some menopause-type symptoms due to fluctuating oestrogen levels.[64]

For trans and non-binary people, any physical symptoms of menopause can exacerbate gender dysmorphia. Meanwhile, trans people are more likely to suffer in silence at work to avoid disclosing their trans status with colleagues.[65]

Male hormone decline

Cisgender men also experience a decline in hormones as they age called andropause. Testosterone typically peaks in a man's 20s and then declines very gradually by about 1% per year after that. Men do not normally experience a sudden, rapid or fluctuating change at any particular stage. Symptoms such as changes in mood, sexual dysfunction, energy, sleep, body fat, bone and muscle strength may begin to emerge in a man's 40s and 50s. They may even experience hot flushes. However, these are usually far less obvious than is the case for women experiencing menopause. Only 2% of men over the age of 40 become so deficient that they require hormone replacement.[66] Symptoms that are more noticeable are normally driven by other health conditions rather than testosterone deficiency alone.[67]

Low testosterone can also occur in younger men because of genetic differences, illness, cancer treatment or problems with the hypothalamus and pituitary glands in the brain. Occasionally, symptoms may be severe and resemble aspects of female menopause, prompting the need for hormone replacement therapy.

Shaken not stirred: managing a cocktail of menopause symptoms

It is hard to get clarity on what menopause is, due to the cocktail of symptoms and huge variability in how these are expressed in different people. Indeed, not every woman will experience noticeable symptoms. Some may even find that menopause brings benefits once periods and the associated fluctuations in hormone levels end. For others, menopause symptoms can be so extreme that they make it impossible to continue a normal lifestyle. For example, some women may suffer debilitating migraines.[68] Others, in extreme cases, may experience psychosis[69] or have increased suicidal intentionality.[70]

Most women will notice at least some negative symptoms as they progress through perimenopause and menopause. Many experience problem symptoms but may not realize these are due to menopause. Research by Newson Health on over 5,000 UK women aged 45–55 years found that nearly all (96%) experienced menopausal symptoms.[71] Three-quarters had been experiencing menopausal symptoms for more than a year (75%), and more than 1 in 7 (15%) had been experiencing symptoms for more than six years.

There is a range of options for managing symptoms and women will find different pathways that suit their needs and preferences. Discovering that path can take time and relies on access to reliable information and the right support. For some, the management of symptoms is dependent on access to HRT. For others, a non-medical holistic approach can work.

In all cases there is a need to understand the challenges that symptoms present in everyday life and to balance the impact of menopause on both body and mind.

What's on the menopause menu?

The process of hormonal decline through perimenopause and up to menopause brings a wide range of physical, emotional and cognitive symptoms. A woman can easily recognize when she has reached menopause. She will have had no period for at least a year. Recognizing that she is perimenopausal and entering the menopause transition is laden with difficulty. Symptoms are different for each person and individuals often don't add up the creeping progression of signs. Doctors may focus on the specific issue the patient presents with and may not see the wider emerging pattern. If the individual is a little younger than the average menopausal age, then there can be a mental block to even considering menopause as an underlying cause.

Although most women (79%) surveyed by Newson Health in 2021[72] went to see a doctor about their symptoms, it was not unusual to require several visits and delays of a year or more until adequate treatment was received. A blind spot with menopause arises partly through ignorance of the multitude of overlapping and interacting symptoms along with an overemphasis on a few particular symptoms, such as hot flushes, that may only emerge later on or not at all for any one individual.

- A lucky 15% of women never have a hot flush.
- A third only have hot flushes when menstruation is about to stop.
- A quarter start hot flushes well before menopause but can look forward to them ending along with last their menstrual cycle.
- A quarter are 'super-flushers' having hot flushes well before and after menopause.[73]

Understanding the menopause transition and its impact | 35

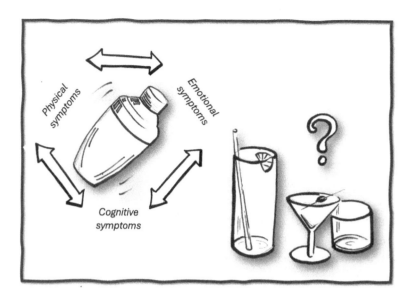

Figure 2.2: Menopause can bring a cocktail of symptoms that is unique for each woman.

Physical symptoms

The physical symptoms of menopause are arguably those that are most widely understood but which may still lie unrecognized for years. Not everyone experiences all of these, but the most common physical symptoms in the UK are changes in bleeding, hot flushes, night sweats, sleep disorders, genitourinary problems, and joint pain.[74] A CIPD study found that around two-thirds of UK working women aged over 40 experience hot flushes (67%), sleep disturbance (66%) and muscle and joint problems (64%).[75]

The list of possible physical symptoms is a long one. Often, they are mistaken for other conditions or explained away by a vague notion of getting older. As physical symptoms often occur alongside emotional ones, too often the physical symptoms are assumed to be psychosomatic and essentially having no concrete somatic cause.

Emotional symptoms

Emotional symptoms can be more prevalent than the physical ones.[76] Women often experience anxiety, low mood or display angry outbursts. They may lose all sense of joy or motivation, or even experience severe mental illness[77] or suicidal thoughts.[78] However, emotional symptoms can be additionally difficult to pin down and may allow menopause to hide in plain sight.

As we see in Chapter 1, menopause most often occurs at a stage in life where there is a lot going on for women. As a result, doctors and women themselves, often put down emotional symptoms to concurrent stressors. Often women are prescribed antidepressants long before and, for that matter, long after menopause has been considered. A survey of 2,920 women by Newson Health found that two-thirds (66%) were prescribed antidepressants after reporting symptoms of menopause.[79] Although antidepressants can be a helpful alternative to HRT for some women,[80] this doesn't address the wide array of physical problems that persist.

Cognitive symptoms

Only now is research beginning to show the intricate relationship between sex hormones and the brain.[81] Separate from physical and emotional impacts, some of the most subtle, and yet frightening, symptoms for women are seen in how people solve problems, make plans or remember things; in other words, their cognitive capabilities.

Time and again we hear of women thinking they have early dementia without any clue that their thinking problems are related to hormones. They may suffer days of severe brain fog, unable to plan and prioritize. They may forget normal everyday words or names and feel unable to express themselves with anything like their usual clarity. At home this might, at times, be amusing. At work they can find their credibility undermined.

Battling through the haze only adds to the stress, creating a vicious cycle that worsens cognitive performance. It is not surprising that women who experience predominantly cognitive or mood-related symptoms, rather than physical, are even more likely to report a negative impact on their working life.[82]

Interaction between symptoms

There are complex interactions between symptoms making it difficult to pinpoint specific causes. For example, perimenopause can trigger a decrease in melatonin, leading to disruption of the circadian rhythms that maintain a normal sleep pattern.[83] However, physical symptoms can also contribute towards sleep disturbance and this, in turn, can exacerbate cognitive symptoms such as a loss of verbal memory[84] as well as affecting long-term physical, emotional and cognitive health.

Sometimes symptoms may be caused by complex interactions between physiology, behaviour and the external environment. For example, depressive symptoms in menopause have been shown to be influenced by a lack of external support in addition to any direct effects of hormone changes, and the knock-on effects of symptoms such as sleep loss.

Cultural and ethnic diversity in symptoms

There is a real risk that our concept of what the menopause transition is like is biased towards a white Western experience. Race, culture and ethnicity all impact women's experiences of menopause.[85] Ethnic diversity not only impacts when menopause starts, but also the types and the severity of symptoms experienced in perimenopause. For example, women in the UK, of African Caribbean origin, experience worse hot flushes and higher sleep disruption.[86] Unfortunately, a lack of understanding means that women of colour can often have their experience of symptoms missed or dismissed.[87]

Some studies suggest that where a culture includes a high soya diet women experience fewer problems with hot flushes,[88] and this is sometimes taken to signify that menopause is less of an issue in those cultures. However, in Singapore, it was shown that women may continue to be challenged in other ways, more commonly experiencing symptoms such as muscle and joint pain.[89]

Table 2.1: Range of symptoms and conditions experienced from perimenopause through to post-menopause.[90,91,92,93]

Physical	Emotional
Allergies	Anger or irritability
Anaemia	Anxiety
Bloating and digestive issues	Reduced confidence
	Fatigue
Feeling dizzy or faint	Loss of joy
Headaches and migraines	Reduced libido
Hair dryness and thinning	Low mood
Heart palpitations	Lack of motivation
Heavier or irregular periods	Mood swings
Hot flushes and night sweats	Panic attacks
	Suicidal thoughts
Joint and muscle pain	Tearfulness
Reduction in bone density	**Cognitive**
Reduction in muscle mass	Difficulty absorbing information
Restless legs	
Skin dryness and itching	Poor concentration
Sleep disorders	Brain fog
Tinnitus	Difficulty with decision-making
UTIs and bladder control issues	
	Forgetfulness
Vaginal or vulval dryness and pain	Reduced information processing speed
Weight gain	Poor verbal memory

I did it my way!

For those who have not experienced menopause or had to search for answers to myriad symptoms, it can be easy to assume that a quick trip to the doctor will provide the answers. Unfortunately, a quick fix is not always available. Each woman's menopause journey – in terms of noticing symptoms, having these recognized as menopause related, and finding and choosing the right treatment options – can be mentally and emotionally draining. This is alongside trying to keep up business as usual.

Options for non-medical management

Where symptoms are minor, simple changes to diet and lifestyle can be enough. For example, managing blood sugar levels, staying hydrated, reducing alcohol consumption, minimizing ultra-processed foods, boosting protein levels and improving gut health can all help women to maintain a healthy weight, raise energy levels, stabilize their mood and improve their response to stress.[94]

Women find exercise critically important around the time of the menopause, for boosting their mood as well as contributing to stronger muscles, bones and metabolism.[95] Strength-building exercise and activities such as yoga that incorporate mindfulness and breath control are recognized as particularly helpful.

Psychological support can be beneficial too in helping women to reframe the changes they are experiencing and find a way forward. There is much to learn from societies where the language around menopause is more positive and where this enables women to maintain a more positive mindset. For example, in Japan the word for menopause is *konenki*, meaning 'season of renewed energy'. Practising a more positive mindset, such as through cognitive behavioural therapy (CBT) has been proven to reduce the severity of symptoms experienced.[96,97]

Hormone replacement therapy

When women suffer more severe symptoms that clash with the demands of everyday life, it may not be possible to keep these sufficiently in check without medical help. It might require more than positive thinking, exercise and a healthy diet to get many women through. Furthermore, the pressures and constraints of working life may make it difficult for women to prioritize exercise, rest and diet as much as would be ideal.

For many women HRT can offer a lifeline with the opportunity to restore natural levels of hormones that have been lost. In this way HRT addresses the symptoms at root cause. Having said that, women do not all respond to HRT in the same way. It is often a process of trial and error to find the right product and dose that addresses a particular woman's symptoms without triggering unhelpful side effects. Also, over time, there may be a need to alter the prescribed HRT as a woman's body continues to change. This means that even with HRT, it can be an ongoing challenge to manage symptoms.

The main hormones that are replaced in HRT are:

- **Oestrogen:** this helps with a wide variety of physical, emotional and cognitive symptoms that emerge in perimenopause and menopause.

- **Progesterone:** when taking oestrogen, this is essential for maintaining a healthy womb-lining. It can also help with mood and sleep.

- **Testosterone:** in the UK, testosterone replacement is not currently licensed for women but may be prescribed for a low libido. There is limited data on the long-term benefits. However, many women taking testosterone report improvements in energy, mood, cognitive function.[98,99,100]

Empowering informed choices

It is important that women can make informed choices that will provide the best pathway for managing their own symptoms, constraints and priorities. Each woman will look to medical experts, menopause well-being specialists, the media and friends to learn about their options. In doing so they may encounter conflicting attitudes, scaremongering and misinformation. In this rapidly developing field, it can be hard to find a way through that balances the benefits and risks of different options. Women need access to knowledgeable and supportive health care providers to help them navigate this and feel empowered to choose a treatment path that is right for them, whether that is medical or non-medical.[101]

Cultural differences play their part in women's access to support. Culture can impact the likelihood of women discussing their symptoms and seeking help in the first place. It can also impact how women's symptoms are perceived by others when they do reach out for help.

Countering unfounded fears

Having decided to use HRT, women must overcome fears about 'messing' with the natural process of menopause. Many people have been strongly influenced by a particular research paper in 2002 by the Women's Health Initiative that linked the use of oestrogen replacement to an increased risk of breast cancer. This dramatically altered women's confidence in using HRT and doctors' readiness to prescribe it. The research had significant flaws: it over-represented much older women in the treatment cohort and utilized synthetic hormones rather than the bio-identical ones preferred today.[102] As older women are more predisposed to breast cancer this made for an unfair comparison. Follow-up studies have shown that oestrogen can have an overall beneficial effect on women's health and can even reduce the risk of breast cancer for some.

Balancing relative risks

Whichever pathway a woman takes for managing her menopause symptoms, there are likely to be a range of relative benefits and risks. Women need accurate information that enables them to make a 'risk versus benefit' analysis for themselves. This is just as they would do when weighing up an oral contraceptive versus a natural method of contraception.

As an example, for women with a uterus, progesterone must be taken concurrently with oestrogen to prevent the oestrogen overstimulating the growth of the lining of the womb. This progesterone, while protecting the womb, can have the potential of raising the risk of breast cancer. However, the risk is so low (Women's Health Initiative (WHI) figures place it at less than 0.001%) that for most women it is far outweighed by the numerous health benefits such as reducing the risk of cardiovascular disease, colon cancer, diabetes and osteoporosis – especially where other health factors are maintained such as exercise, not smoking and low alcohol consumption.

Identifying personal priorities

Attitudes towards the options for managing symptoms vary considerably. Although there is increasingly compelling evidence that HRT delivers more benefit than harm for women, it is important that women are given agency to decide what feels right for them. Any one of the following viewpoints is valid and to be celebrated as an expression of an individual's preferences and rights.

> ▶ Some women may hold a personal commitment to taking a more 'natural' route and feel a greater sense of empowerment in achieving hormonal balance without the help of HRT. They may wish to resist the over-medicalization of women's bodies.

- ▶ Some may try HRT but feel unhappy with side-effects that HRT can trigger for them and feel that the search for the perfect doses only adds to the pressures they are under.

- ▶ Other women don't see the point of depriving themselves of HRT, challenging the view that, as women, they are destined always to soldier on when they could, instead, truly thrive.

- ▶ Some women could manage fine without HRT, but are convinced of the long-term health benefits of HRT for their bodies and brains.

- ▶ Many are happy to take a holistic approach and introduce lifestyle changes alongside HRT.

Navigating different healthcare providers

Where women *do* seek HRT, they must navigate a range of attitudes and expertise from healthcare providers too. Some are eager to provide access to hormones viewing this as preventative medicine. Others may be extremely reluctant to turn to HRT and may doubt a woman's need for medical support with symptoms at all.[103]

Not every doctor will share the same training and awareness. A survey in 2021 showed that only 41% of UK medical degree courses had mandatory training on menopause.[104] Where training *does* exist, it may not be sufficient for non-typical cases. If a woman has a more complicated medical history that changes the balance of risk, deeper specialist advice may be needed. Even then, those who do specialize in menopause may be limited by the availability of reliable data.

A major limiting factor is the amount of time a health professional can offer. A typical NHS GP appointment in the UK is 10 minutes. This makes it very difficult for a patient to communicate their complex symptoms and needs, and for the doctor to ensure an empowering patient-centred approach towards menopause.

How menopause puts the breaks on women at work

So, the facts are in. Menopausal women have a lot to contend with. The question is, why is this relevant for organizations? Some women might sail through menopause without any significant direct consequence for their work. Nevertheless, the mild symptoms they do experience can be compounded by all the 'stuff' they have going on outside of work. This can mean that women reach a tipping point in their relationship to their work. For others, menopause wreaks havoc on their bodies and minds, sometimes suddenly and dramatically, sometimes for several years.

A study of over 8,800 women in the United States found that those experiencing menopausal symptoms had significantly lower levels of health-related quality of life and significantly higher work impairment.[105] As a result, we see negative consequences for women's participation, performance, progression and well-being at work.

Despite the very real threat this poses to women's careers, they remain unlikely to tell their bosses, preferring to keep symptoms and the cause of symptoms hidden. Where women do not feel safe to disclose, this increases the levels of stress and the impact of menopause symptoms is worsened.

When symptoms and work collide

Menopause symptoms not only impact how women feel about work, they can also translate into women's participation, performance, progression and well-being.

In 2023, the CIPD published a survey of 2000 working women aged 40–60 in the UK. This illustrated the prevalence of menopause symptoms experienced by working women through their own perceptions of how this had impacted them at work. Nearly 9 in 10 (88%) of those aged 51–60 were experiencing or had experienced menopause symptoms. Nearly 3 in 10 (57%) of those aged 40–50 said the same.[106] Negative impacts related to women's ability to concentrate, and to cope psychologically, interpersonally or physically with the demands they faced at work. Over half of the women had, at least once, taken time off work due to their symptoms; around a quarter (23%) had considered leaving work; or had experienced a negative impact on their career progression (27%).

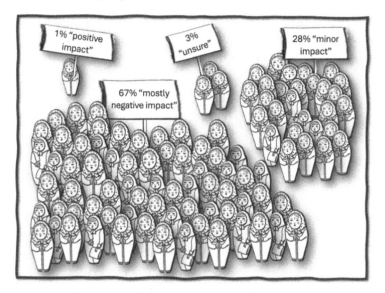

Figure 2.3: How different women are impacted by menopause symptoms at work.

Source: Bazeley, Marren, Shepherd and Fawcett Society (2002).

A 2022 study commissioned by Channel 4 with support from the Fawcett Society interviewed More than 4,000 women aged 45–55 who were currently, or had in the past, experienced menopause symptoms.[107] (Note that data excluded those experiencing menopause in younger or older age groups, and excluded trans and non-binary people.) Of those in the target group, 44% said their ability to work had been affected, with 61% saying they had lost motivation at work and 52% saying they had lost confidence.

This has consequences for women's readiness for additional challenge at work: 8% said they had not applied for a promotion due to their menopause symptoms and 4% had turned down a promotion. Women often felt they must reduce their hours (14%) or go part-time (14%) in order to cope.

Although the limitations in this study make it unreliable to extrapolate to the population as a whole, 1 in 10 of those included in the Fawcett study had left employment altogether due to their menopause symptoms. For those who experienced five or more 'very difficult' symptoms from menopause, the proportion who left work doubled.

More academically rigorous studies reached similar conclusions. One longitudinal study, following a cohort of women through from childhood (data from the National Child Development Survey)[108] found that at the age of 50, those with more severe menopausal symptoms were significantly more likely to have left employment (11.2% in total had left employment; those with severe symptoms were 43% more likely to have left work than their counterparts).[109] They were also more likely to have reduced their hours of employment (23.2% in total had reduced their weekly working hours; but women with severe symptoms were 23% more likely to have done so). In another study, using the same data set, researchers found that whilst all women in the study showed a rapid decline in their employment rate in their 50s, the decline was much steeper for those who had experienced natural menopause under the age of 45, with this latter group 9% less likely to still be in employment.[110]

Participate

↓ 23% considered leaving or left work*
↓ 10% left employment**
↓ 43% increase in leaving work if symptoms severe***
↓ 9% higher decline in employment rate following early menopause***
↓ 14% reduced their hours**
↓ 23% increase in reducing hours if symptoms severe***

* CIPD survey of 2000 working women aged 40-60 in the UK, 2023
** Fawcett Society survey of 4000 women aged 45-55 with experience of menopause symptoms
*** Study of >3000 women aged 50, using data from the National Child Development Study (NCDS)
**** Study of >3400 women aged 50 who had experienced natural menopause without HRT treatment using data from the NCDS.

Perform

↓ 79% less able to concentrate*
↓ 61% lost motivation**
↓ 44% ability to work affected at some point**

Progress

↓ 27% experience negative impact on career progression*
↓ 8% not applied for promotion**
↓ 4% said no to offer of promotion**

Thrive

↓ 53% taken time off*
↓ 52% lost confidence**
↓ 69% report anxiety or depression**

Figure 2.4: Reported impact on work outcomes for women experiencing menopause symptoms.

There's no easy fix for menopause symptoms. The timings, severity and combination of symptoms can vary enormously between individuals but most often there are negative consequences for women's participation, performance, progression and well-being at work. Taking action on menopause starts with understanding the menopause transition and its impact at work.

Key themes in Chapter 2

1. Sex hormones are important for everyone's health and well-being over and above their role in reproduction.

2. It is common for women to experience menopause symptoms due to chaotic or rapid changes that can occur in the menopause transition.

3. The type, severity and length of time of symptoms is unique for each woman and can vary across cultures and ethnicities.

4. Transgender employees and cisgender men can also experience symptoms from hormonal change.

5. There is a range of medical and non-medical options for managing symptoms.

6. Women benefit when empowered to balance treatment options and risks in a way that works for them, supported by evidence.

7. With or without treatment, symptoms can directly impact women's participation, performance, progression and well-being at work.

3
Why menopause-friendly organizations deliver value

Making an organization menopause-friendly requires time and effort to turn the tide on old established practices. Leaders may well believe that it is simply the right thing to do with a broad social return, and therefore an expense that must be covered. However, to justify any investment, and the disruptiveness of change, it helps to identify a strong business case. With so many organizations benefitting from menopause actions, momentum continues to grow. Organizations that are not participating in change will find themselves left behind if they do not embrace menopause-friendly practices.

In this chapter, I outline the business case for taking action on menopause. I look at the positive pay-off of instituting change, and the relative costs of doing nothing. I show how a menopause action plan can be vitally important in helping an organization achieve its strategic mission with clear financial returns. I also show the potential to add ethical capital that further strengthens an organization's brand value and attract investors, customers and talent.

Securing a strategic, financial and ethical pay-off

Quite simply 'it pays' to be more menopause friendly, delivering clear strategic gains for organizations. Having a more diverse workforce that includes older women enables organizations to better deliver their vision, with increased commercial success and service improvement. Unless an organization is menopause friendly, it will miss out on opportunities to attract, develop, retain and optimize older female talent.[111] In a world where other organizations are already doing this successfully, there is the potential to be left behind.[112,113]

While it pays to be menopause friendly, it is also the right thing to do. Organizations are seeing this as an important element of being a responsible employer and a powerful way to make a positive contribution to society. Of course, ethical brands deliver financial value too, creating a circular benefit.

Talent attraction and retention

Doing nothing was more acceptable in the past as there were comparatively few women of menopausal age still in work. However, with changing demographics at work (see Chapter 1), there is increasing utility in maximizing the value of older women in the workplace. Organizations might look at menopause in relation to the 'extensive margin costs' that could be incurred, with the absence of menopause-friendly practices resulting in a failure to attract, recruit and retain women's labour.

Costs vary depending on the sector and the need to maximize the participation of older women.[114] Some sectors, such as health, social care, teaching, retail, banking and finance, rely heavily on a female workforce.[115,116] So here there is a particularly strong case for securing and maintaining the hours worked by older women. This is particularly true where the sector is already struggling to recruit and retain staff such as in health and social care.[117] In fact, menopause has been estimated to cost the NHS between £89 million and £129 million every year.[118]

Other sectors may be more male dominated but struggle to recruit and retain people with the right skills. For example, within IT and technology, more than half the women who join the industry will leave within the first 10 to 20 years due to issues such as limited career prospects and experiences of discrimination.[119] This is double the rate of attrition for men. The benefit for tech organizations of holding onto female talent through to later careers is enormous if they are to meet their growth ambitions and service commitments.

If women leave work as a result of their experience of menopause, or reduce their participation through opting for part-time working, this brings measurable costs for employers. Increased costs from recruiting and training new hires can be significant. The average financial cost of losing just one employee earning £25,000 ranged from £20,000 to £40,000 depending on the sector.[120] However, menopausal women often leave at the peak of their careers, and just as they are taking up more senior management roles. The cost of sourcing and developing equivalent senior talent is far higher.

Improved participation	Improved performance	Improved progression	Improved well-being
Attracting staff	Higher productivity	Maximizing potential	Delivering social responsibility
Retaining staff	Improved quality	Diversity at all levels	Reduced absenteeism
Working more hours	Stronger teamwork	Lower gender pay gap	Lower occupational health risks

Figure 3.1: The payoff for menopause friendly actions.

Performance and talent optimization

Menopause-friendly practices can play an important role in wider talent optimization, ensuring that an organization not only attracts and keeps older women but that they get the full value from this employee group. The impact can be evaluated in terms of minimizing the 'intensive margin costs' related to menopause.[121]

Menopause-friendly practices can help women to sustain performance and be more productive in their existing roles. By offering more support, and the right culture and environment, organizations can lessen the negative impact of symptoms. This means women are more likely to sustain their focus and energy and perform more consistently at their full potential. They may also be less likely to take sick leave, lessening the impact on colleagues. Newson Health found that 59% of women surveyed via an online questionnaire had taken time off work due to menopause symptoms and 18% reported that they were off for more than eight weeks.[122]

On paper an organization might employ a large number of women but at the same time see women under-represented in more senior roles. Without the right support, women experiencing menopause may hold back from further challenge and progression opportunities, exacerbating a lack of senior diversity. Organizations with menopause-friendly strategies, on the other hand, will find ways to motivate and develop their older female talent securing far greater long-term value and impact from that talent as this talent progresses.

Menopause-friendly organizations give older women a place at the table to contribute their valuable perspective to decisions and to voice alternative ideas. There is strong evidence of the value for diverse teams in decision-making. Unfortunately, senior leadership teams very often lack a female perspective. This matters as women will often bring different life experiences, different attitudes to risk and different motivations that help to balance the strategic decision made at a senior level. A report for Credit Suisse Research in 2012 found that companies with at least one woman on the board outperformed those with none in terms of growth (14% versus 10%), share price, return on equity (16% versus 12%), lower leverage and higher valuations (2.4x versus 1.8x).[123] The benefit was particularly important during the period of the financial crisis. The uplift in performance was put down to men on the board stepping up their effort with the presence of a senior female colleague; women bringing additional leadership skills that the senior team lacks, the recruitment of women opening up access to a wider talent pool; organizations being able to better reflect the concerns of female customers and service users; women exhibiting a stronger focus on corporate governance; and women's different attitudes to risk.

Older women represent a valuable demographic among customers and service users. Organizations that give menopausal women a voice will be more able to shape and respond to the needs of this group. As women's economic independence has evolved, so has their individual buying power. One industry that understands the potential for this is in motor manufacturing. Jaguar Land Rover cites that 85% of car-buying decisions are influenced by women.[124] They have shaped their equity, diversity and inclusion (EDI) strategies to ensure the company better reflect the needs and perspectives of female customers.

With older women representing a vital and growing cohort of employees, there's an increasingly significant advantage to be gained for organizations by becoming more menopause friendly. Doing nothing to proactively attract and engage older women represents a huge missed opportunity in terms of improved retention, productivity, performance and well-being.

Sustaining an ethical brand

Menopause-friendly organizations are not only motivated by the financial gains to be won. Alongside commercial and service targets many organizations will also prioritize being good employers and citizens, even where the investment possibly exceeds the measurable gains. Increasingly, organizations – both in the public and private sectors – are aiming to secure a social return on investment (SROI) and 'account for the social, economic and environmental value that results from their activities.'[125]

In reality, it is impossible to separate an organization's corporate social responsibility (CSR) credentials from any resulting commercial gain. Increasingly these are intertwined so that organizations reap rewards for doing good things. CSR practices are linked to improved financial returns, increasing the market value of organizations by 4–6%; increasing valuations for companies with strong stakeholder relationship by 40–80%; and increasing revenue by up to 20%.[126] CSR commitments change how the organization is regarded by investors, customers and by potential employees. A YouGov survey tracker reported that nearly half of British people would not buy from a brand that treated staff badly, and a further third would think less of the brand.[127] This highlights the critical value of CSR and EDI practices in preserving brand value. Employer brand is also increasingly critical for attracting top talent. In a study by BUPA, 31% of Gen Z workers would turn down a role in a company that had a poor ESG record, and 22% list corporate values as their leading concern in choosing a new role.[128] Where organizations compete for the best people, having a strong employer brand is, therefore, a vital differentiator.

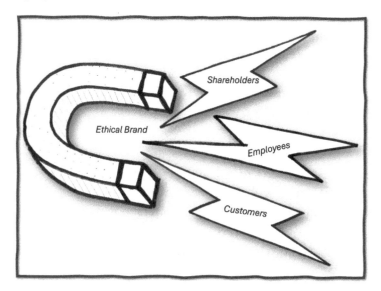

Figure 3.2: Ethical brands act as a magnet attracting customers, employees and shareholders.

Securing the benefits of stronger EDI

Having a genuine commitment towards menopause will sit within an organization's wider aims around EDI. This goes beyond legal compliance and doing the minimum to avoid litigation. It also goes beyond simply appearing to do the right things in order to boost a brand message. Rather, it speaks to a core belief in the value of providing fairness and opportunity to a broad spectrum of people and creating an environment where everyone has an equitable chance to perform, progress, be rewarded and thrive. What signifies 'doing the right thing' has complexity. The public and political backlash against what is perceived by some as a 'woke' agenda demonstrates the power of perspective when we resort to moral arguments. Nevertheless, many organizations seek a sense of purpose through the promotion of shared egalitarian values.

Organizational justice benefits people and organizations as it can build trust and minimize conflict which leads to better employee engagement and performance. When treated with justice, employees are also more likely to engage in citizenship behaviours, complying with workplace policies, behaving more altruistically towards colleagues, and engaging positively with service users or customers. Therefore, there is a strong utilitarian argument for adopting what some might see as philosophical or moralistic principles.

There are three key elements to organizational justice.[129] These are directly relevant to the policies and practices we adopt around EDI and will impact an organization's strategies for menopause: procedural justice; interactional justice; and distributive justice:

1. **Procedural justice** relates to making consistent, unbiased decisions. It would be hard for anyone to argue against the importance of objectivity in making fair decisions. This impacts how we hire, develop, share roles, reward, etc. Few would wish decisions to be arbitrary or to openly facilitate favouritism. It can nevertheless be a challenge to achieve this as bias is often woven into the fabric of how employee decisions are made.

2. **Interactional justice** relates to treating others with honesty, respect and dignity. Again, few would disagree and endorse treating particular groups with disrespect. Interactional justice plays a fundamental role in ensuring that all individuals can give their best at work. This principle can be difficult to implement where, for example, sensitivities around humour and language are felt by others to infringe on their personal freedom of expression.

3. **Distributive justice** relates to sharing equitable opportunities and outcomes – who gets what and why. It can be harder to gain consensus on this as it hinges on the concept of what is equitable and the extent to which one takes a wider view that goes beyond what is observed within an organization in the here and now. This can be a particular sticking point when addressing systemic inequality as organizations may tacitly maintain the status quo that has benefited particular groups in the past.

It's worth delving into point 3 a little more. 'Equity' is not the same as 'treating everyone the same'. Resistance to EDI strategies often revolves around our understanding of equity, and when and why we might need to exercise this rather than only offer equality. To be equitable, we have to ensure that opportunities and outcomes are shared in a way that evens out any pre-existing advantage and disadvantage established through historical, and potentially outdated, practices. It takes a longer-term view that considers what could be as well as what is. We might do this by weighing up the following:[130]

- **Merit:** what is deserved relative to what someone delivers or could deliver. Many passionately argue that organizations should treat people on merit alone. Very often they will be thinking of merit in terms of what people have actually delivered. However, if we only focus on what someone delivers now, then we may miss out on the value of their longer-term potential. This potential may be yet untapped due to differences in opportunity and experience that the person has encountered to date. Therefore, it can be argued that it is fair to broaden our understanding of merit beyond what can be observed today and to include potential for the future.

- **Equality:** what offers an equal chance of success versus simply an equal opportunity. This requires us to offer extra support and resources to some, in order to counter systemic unfairness that may be holding them back through no fault of their own. Through this we provide a means for developing their untapped potential.

▶ **Need:** the minimum standards of resources and treatment that everyone can reasonably expect. What someone needs is subjective and driven by individual and cultural context. However, it is helpful for an organization to assume a baseline standard they are willing to uphold and which ensures no group's fundamental rights are denied. For example, a need for physical safety.

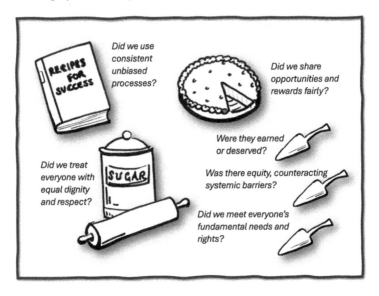

Figure 3.3: Key measures of organizational justice.

Applying this to women experiencing menopause, we would be looking for older women to be treated fairly in decisions that impact their recruitment, reward and progression. We would be working to ensure such decisions were not impacted by bias, but fully recognized women's true capability and also their potential to deliver impact and value in the future. We would be looking for older women to be treated with dignity so that their performance and potential are not unfairly undermined.

We would be looking for ways to open up opportunities so that women can continue to participate, perform, progress and thrive despite health and life-stage challenges. We would be offering additional measures and support to meet individual needs and in recognition of the historical systemic unfairness that disadvantages women.

Managing the risk of legal challenge

An employer may not proactively embrace the opportunities that come through creating a menopause-friendly workplace. However, this poses risks. As legal protections for women tighten and women become more aware of their rights, the chances of litigation grow. Where employers have not taken reasonable steps around menopause, this can be costly in three ways: financial, resources and reputational.

1. **Financial:** employers may incur fees if they seek legal representation. However, if a complaint is upheld then UK tribunals will also award compensation to be paid to employees. In the case of discrimination, there is no statutory limit to the compensation that could be awarded. Increasingly, menopause discrimination claims are being made on the basis of disability and disability discrimination can warrant some of the highest awards, with an average of £26,000 (2021/22).[131]

2. **Resources:** as well as being financially costly, legal challenges can take a long time to resolve. During this time staff will be tied up with gathering evidence and responding to legal queries, which is both time-consuming and emotionally draining.

3. **Reputational:** reputational damage is almost certainly the biggest cost of all if a legal challenge is successful.[132] The media is showing increasing interest in cases related to menopause, with coverage likely to be picked up via national news channels and then spread virally online.

How the law is becoming less 'grey' on menopause

There may be times where menopause has sufficient impact on the individual's capability or conduct to justify the employer taking action, possibly even dismissal. Each case would depend on the specific facts. However, employers could find they have to defend themselves against claims of discrimination on the grounds of sex, age or disability arising due to menopause symptoms, under the terms of the Equality Act 2010. Furthermore, to avoid a successful claim of unfair dismissal, the employer might need to demonstrate they have acted fairly and followed proper process, in keeping with the Employment Rights Act 1996.

In the UK, legislation has been in place for some time that affords employees protection from unfair treatment. However, as the number of women experiencing menopause grows within the workplace, the effectiveness of the law and our understanding of how it applies to this group is developing. Menopause can be a somewhat 'grey' area legally, but case law is helping to make protections clearer and more robust for women experiencing menopause.

In fact, an increasing number of women are now looking to the law to make claims against their employer rather than suffer in silence. Data from HM Courts & Tribunal Service show that the number of employment tribunal decisions relating to menopause has multiplied from five in 2017, to 34 in 2023.[133] Although the numbers are small, we can safely assume this is the tip of the iceberg with many more cases being settled before reaching court. This number is only likely to grow as women with legitimate cases become aware of the possibility of winning claims.

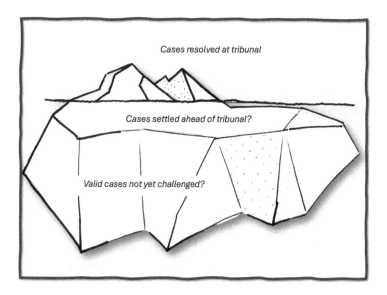

Figure 3.4: The cases resolved at tribunal are likely to be just the tip of the iceberg in potential claims relating to menopause.

The precedent set by UK case law and evolving guidance from the UK government underlines how critical it is that employers take care in fulfilling their legal obligations towards those experiencing menopause.

In the UK, the Equality Act 2010 protects employees against discrimination relating to the following protected characteristics:

- age
- disability
- gender reassignment
- marriage and civil partnership
- pregnancy and maternity
- race
- religion or belief
- sex
- sexual orientation.

Successful claims have been made relating to menopause under three of these characteristics: age, sex and now more frequently, disability.[134] It is also feasible to link menopause claims to gender reassignment. However, due to the wide variability of menopausal symptoms for women of different ages and also across trans communities, there can be difficulties in making a successful claim on the basis of age and sex. Menopause cannot be upheld as age discrimination if it can be shown that older men are not also treated unfavourably, and it cannot be upheld as sex discrimination if it can be shown that younger women are not also treated unfavourably. If a claim relates to disability, then the claimant can also make a claim relating to another characteristic as part of the same proceedings, but the two claims will be determined separately by an employment tribunal. It is not possible, currently, to make a case on the basis of combined characteristics, i.e. that someone has been treated less favourably on the basis of being *both* older and a woman, or on the basis of being *both* disabled and a woman (although as we will hear, this may change).

To date, there has been greater success in the UK in relating menopause claims to the single characteristic of 'disability'. Many menopause symptoms can be transient or vary in severity from woman to woman and most women may not regard themselves as having a disability when experiencing menopause. However, it is perfectly feasible for an individual to evidence that her menopausal symptoms deliver a 'long-term and substantial impact' on her ability to carry out normal day-to-day activities – the legal definition of a disability.

> ### Case study: Rooney vs Leicester City Council 2021
>
> The employee worked as a childcare social worker for 12 years until she resigned. She claimed her resignation was partly due to the lack of support given in relation to her menopause symptoms. For two years she had suffered a range of symptoms such as poor sleep, headaches, hot flushes, emotional and cognitive symptoms, and had evidence of seeking medical treatment. Her claim for harassment and victimization on the grounds of disability was initially refused as the tribunal decided this did not constitute a disability. However, on appeal it was found that the original tribunal had not taken sufficient account of what the claimant couldn't do as a result of her menopause symptoms. At a new tribunal, it was decided that the impact of her symptoms did constitute a disability, as they were 'more than minor or trivial', and as they had persisted more than a year could be considered 'long-term'.[135]

In the USA, the law lags behind the UK in terms of protections for women experiencing menopause. As a result, there have been few cases in the America. According to Cahn et al., in 2023[136] 'no federal law requires employers to accommodate menopausal symptoms'. There are protections for disabilities. However, cases that have attempted to have menopause treated legally as a disability have failed. Attempts to make a claim of sex discrimination relating to menopause symptoms have also hit difficulties.

> **Case study: Coleman vs Bobby Dodd Institute 2017**
>
> The employee had been sacked as a result of two incidents where her heavy bleeding had leaked onto furnishings. The courts dismissed her claim. However, Coleman did, nevertheless, secure an undisclosed settlement.

Possible changes to UK law

At the time of writing (2024), the new Labour Government in the UK is proposing changes to the law that will enable a claim to be made on the basis of 'combined' (dual) discrimination.[137] This will strengthen protection for older women experiencing menopause where a unique intersection between age, sex and disability characteristics can underly discrimination. Combined discrimination claims may also come into play in the future for ethnic minority women whose menopause experience could result in differential treatment at work, or for trans men who might experience discrimination relating to menopause alongside discrimination related to gender reassignment.

Another change proposed in the UK is to extend existing equal pay legislation to race and disability. Currently it only applies to differences in pay based on sex. It can be a difficult and lengthy process bringing an equal pay claim and there may be challenges in implementing this proposed change to the law.[138] However, this change could increase the potential for an equal pay claim for women experiencing pay discrimination on the basis of the health consequences for menopause.

The low-down on UK discrimination law

With or without the proposed changes mentioned earlier, there is a range of scenarios that could potentially create the basis for a legal claim from someone experiencing menopause. These fall under the categories of direct, and indirect discrimination[139] and harassment,[140] which are prohibited for all protected characteristics. Discrimination can also occur where the employee is disadvantaged or treated less favourably due to an association with a characteristic rather than because they, themselves, possess the characteristic. For example, a younger person experiencing menopause could feasibly still claim age discrimination if they experience inappropriate humour that ridicules their menopause experience.[141]

Direct discrimination could be claimed where an individual is treated 'less favourably' specifically because of having a protected characteristic and any real or assumed impact related to that. For example, someone may have been excluded from a promotion as they were perceived to be menopausal and therefore assumed to be past their peak performance years without any actual evidence of this being true for that individual. In response to a claim, possibly of age discrimination, the employer would need to provide evidence that the individual had not been treated less favourably than a comparator who did not share the same protected characteristic.

Indirect discrimination could be claimed where there is a blanket rule, practice or treatment that applies to everyone, but which creates unfair disadvantage for anyone who shares a certain protected characteristic. For example, limited access to toilet facilities may have created additional discomfort and impacted well-being or performance for those experiencing menopausal symptoms. In response to a claim, possibly of sex discrimination, the employer would need to provide evidence that there had been no 'particular disadvantage' created for people in the group sharing this protected characteristic relative to those outside the group.

Case study: Lynskey vs Direct Line Insurance Services 2022

The employee was given a low appraisal rating and a written warning for performance. She also had sick pay removed without warning. Her claim of discrimination on the grounds of disability was upheld as the employer could not demonstrate that they had taken sufficient account of her menopause symptoms. She was awarded just under £65,000 in damages for failure to make reasonable adjustments.[142]

Harassment could be claimed where a person receives unwanted conduct from another individual at work in relation to a protected characteristic and where this conduct has the purpose of violating that person's dignity or of creating an intimidating, hostile, degrading, humiliating or offensive environment. For example, if a colleague's jokes relating to menopause undermined someone's sense of dignity, this has the potential to lead to a claim of harassment on the basis of age or sex. In this case, the onus is on the claimant to demonstrate that the behaviour was unwanted, that it related to a protected characteristic and that it had the impact of violating their dignity.

Case study: Best vs Embark on Raw Ltd 2006

An employee who worked as a sales assistant was dismissed on the basis of alleged rude and confrontational behaviour with colleagues. During a heated exchange the business owner had made derogatory remarks about the employee's age and the likelihood that she was experiencing menopausal symptoms. The employee's claim of harassment on the grounds of age and also on the grounds of sex was upheld. She was awarded £20,000.[143]

Case study: A. vs Bonmarche Ltd 2019

The employee had worked in retail for 37 years but her work deteriorated when she started to experience symptoms of menopause. Her manager would ridicule and demean her in front of colleagues and refused to make reasonable adjustments to the working environment. She was not supported when she lodged a complaint and ultimately suffered a breakdown. She continued to be treated unfavourably on her return to work and felt forced to resign. The tribunal upheld her claim for unfair dismissal and sex and age discrimination. She was awarded £28,000.[144]

Case study: Farquharson vs Thistle Marine 2023

The employee was an office manager who had been experiencing severe symptoms including heavy bleeding, anxiety and brain fog. When she had worked from home due to her symptoms, she was accused of using menopause as an excuse and told to 'get on with it'. When she raised a grievance about the comments made, her access to the company systems was cut off. This meant she could no longer work from home and pushed her to resign. The tribunal upheld her claim of unfair dismissal and harassment. She was awarded £37,000.[145]

Disability and the right to reasonable adjustments

Additional employment protections are in place specifically in relation to disability. These can be particularly useful for those experiencing menopause. Workers are protected from discrimination not only as a direct result of being disabled but also as a result of something that arises as a consequence of their disability. For example, a woman's menopause symptoms could lead to a series of absences from work. An employer might, unfairly, treat the absences as purely a performance issue (their standard approach for repeated short-term absences) and feel justified in dismissing the employee. However, if the employer could reasonably be expected to have understood that the employee was suffering menopause symptoms, and that these symptoms may amount to a disability under the Equality Act 2010, the employer would need to take extra care to justify any actions taken against the employee.

There is some onus on the employee to disclose their disability in order for this protection to be triggered. However, there may be good reasons for non-disclosure and an employer may still be expected to make assumptions about the potential for menopause-related symptoms to amount to a disability and to act accordingly.

Case study: Davies vs Scottish Courts and Tribunal Service 2018

The employee worked in the tribunal service and disrupted proceedings when she believed two court attendees may have drunk some water in which she may have dissolved her medication for cystitis. This resulted in a verbal altercation in court. Subsequently it was shown that the water did not contain her medication, which would have been evident due to a lack of colouration. The incident resulted in her dismissal as it was decided her behaviour constituted

> gross misconduct. However, her claim for unfair dismissal on the basis of disability discrimination was successful. It was upheld that her menopause symptoms could be considered a disability and the impact on her forgetfulness and behaviour had not been sufficiently considered. She was awarded £19,000 and had her job re-instated.[146]

Where the employer recognizes that an employee is suffering a substantial disadvantage as a result of a disability, by rights the employer should be making 'reasonable adjustments' to remove the disadvantage experienced. This disadvantage may occur as a result of a rule or practice, or physical feature of the working environment. The employee must take reasonable steps to remove the source of the disadvantage or provide an 'auxiliary aid' that ameliorates the disadvantage. The UK Government and Equality and Human Rights Commission (EHRC) provide guidance on a wide range of possible adjustments that can be offered to address disadvantage experienced as a result of menopause. However, it is risky to assume blanket solutions for all individuals experiencing menopause owing to the wide range of varying impacts.

Flexible working from Day One

Some updates to the UK's Employment Rights Act 1996 apply to all workers, but are particularly helpful for employees experiencing difficulties at work due to menopause. In particular, from April 2024, every UK employee was granted the statutory right to request flexible working from their first day of employment.

Flexible working includes a range of options such as: the hours and days worked, start and finish times, the concentration of hours into certain days or times of the year or flexitime. It can also include options for sharing jobs or sharing rostering across teams. However, it isn't just about *when* you work; it also covers *where* you work, such as home-working and hybrid working. With this legislation in place, it becomes much more likely that women experiencing menopause will feel licensed to request flexibility to manage the impact of any symptoms.

Employees must state details of what change they are requesting but are not required to give a reason for the request. Employers are duty-bound to consider such requests in a reasonable manner. Furthermore, employers are expected to agree to requests for flexible working unless they can demonstrate one of a set of eight specific business reasons not to, such as:

1. Burden of additional costs
2. Inability to re-organize staff
3. Inability to recruit additional staff
4. Detrimental impact to quality
5. Detrimental impact to performance
6. Ability to meet customer demand
7. Insufficient work available in the times the employee requests to work
8. Planned structural changes to the employer's business[147]

The right to request flexible working means that any woman could make such a request as a result of menopause without disclosing menopause as the reason. If, however, a woman discloses that her menopause symptoms constitute a disability, the employer has a legal duty to make reasonable adjustments that remove the disadvantage experienced as a result of that disability (in line with the Equality Act 2010). Reasonable adjustments could include flexible working and so, in this case, there is a greater pressure on the employer to grant any flexibility requested.

Menopause as a health and safety issue

Separate from protection from the Equality Act, the UK Health and Safety regulations require employers to conduct a workplace risk assessment and to make reasonable adjustments that protect the health and well-being of their employees at work. This could mean introducing specific reasonable adjustments for those experiencing menopause and ensuring that work and working conditions are conducive to the worker's well-being. Research shows that a poor working environment or conditions have the potential to worsen a woman's menopause symptoms. Therefore, theoretically, the Health and Safety Executive (HSE) could take action against an employer where they have failed in their duty to assess and respond to risks from menopause.

Case study: Shearer vs South Lanarkshire Council 2023

A teacher raised an objection to a proposed move to another school on the basis it would worsen cardiovascular, psychological and menopause symptoms she was experiencing. An occupational health assessment concurred that a move to the proposed school would negatively impact the employee's psychological health. A further psychological risk assessment was completed, but the head teacher did not engage sufficiently with the issue over the subsequent six months. When the employee was later signed off work on long-term sickness absence, her employment was eventually terminated on the basis of capability. She subsequently brought a successful claim for unfair dismissal and disability discrimination. The employee was awarded £61,000.[148]

There is a strong business case for making an organization more menopause friendly. Commercially it pays to take action, with improved attraction, retention and talent optimization. It also can play a key role in sustaining an ethical brand and delivering EDI commitments. Finally, it can be a route to minimizing the risk of legal action and the costs and reputational damage associated with that.

> ### Key themes in Chapter 3
>
> 1. A menopause action plan delivers a range of strategic, financial and ethical pay-offs. It will help every organization to:
>   a. maximize participation by attracting and retaining valuable talent, with more of that talent sustaining a full-time commitment,
>   b. optimize talent with individuals performing, progressing and thriving to their full potential, and
>   c. maintain a strong ethical brand and fulfil EDI commitments.
> 2. Doing nothing on menopause represents a missed opportunity for an organization. However, it also increases the risk of legal action with potential costs and reputational damage.
> 3. Employment law relating to menopause will vary by country and is subject to possible changes in legislation. Within the UK case law is developing and offering greater clarity.
> 4. It pays for managers to be aware of any legal duties relating to menopause. However, expert advice may be needed on specific cases.

4
Focal points for change

There is good evidence that, as a result of menopause, a 'silent ceiling' persists for women in their careers.[149] Although we are now beginning to challenge this silence, we continue to find it a difficult subject to talk about. This allows the problems to perpetuate, and leaves women struggling on their own. Women are not, in themselves, the issue. The difficulties arise when older women encounter a working world that wasn't designed with them in mind. Organizations have an important role to play in helping women feel empowered and able to keep participating, performing, progressing and thriving. We can draw on best practice in the field along with insights from psychology and organizational theory to identify actions that deliver meaningful change.

In this chapter, I outline the factors that perpetuate our silence about menopause and that create a barrier to change in the workplace. I then look at the importance of taking a systems-thinking approach and recognizing the dynamic interaction between women's needs and the way work is designed. I explore the drivers of psychological empowerment that a strong menopause action plan must deliver.

Turning taboo into 'Wow! Who knew?!'

Talking about menopause is difficult. We can find it hard to overcome feelings of embarrassment, shame and stigma or to discuss issues that threaten women's desire to be taken seriously as equals. We might lack the knowledge and language to do this sensitively. However, our silence means that we continue to perpetuate systemic issues that hold women back from positive change. Breaking the taboo around menopause is the critical first step on an organization's menopause journey. This requires us to shine a light on menopause; to replace negative stereotypes with more positive identities; to normalize conversations about ageing and health; and to dare to be honest about the real impact that hormones may have in people's working lives.

Can we have a light here please?

The public discourse on menopause has made enormous strides in raising awareness and breaking the taboo surrounding menopause. Nevertheless, a wall of silence persists which is underpinned by ignorance. As a result, women struggling with a myriad of symptoms may not recognize that the onset of menopause could be driving these and may be woefully unprepared for how they might impact their lives. If menopause has been taboo, the language is often just not there to enable women to articulate what they are experiencing. Very often this leaves women unable to ask for help that they may desperately need.

Women may feel lost and confused about menopause and, as we heard in Chapter 2, they may also fail to get clear consistent answers from the doctors they consult. Medical research has historically excluded women's bodies, leaving doctors woefully under-informed of a woman's physical reality[150] and dismissive of any need to address common women's issues. A lack of consistent advice from doctors around menopause can be deeply unsettling for women and adds to the stress surrounding their experience. Too often women don't think to mention menopause to their GP. Too often their GP doesn't think to mention it either, as happened to me for some years. This allows the symptoms and their impact on women's working lives to continue unchecked.

If women themselves are confused by what they are experiencing, and doctors are confused about how symptoms can and should be treated, it is hardly surprising that colleagues are confused about what menopause means in a work context. At best, this leaves line managers and workmates unsure about what to say, unsure about how to help and uncomfortable in revealing their lack of understanding. At worst, it leads to colleagues sharing inappropriate jokes, dismissive remarks and contributing to a hostile and degrading culture for women experiencing menopause. A lack of supportive dialogue worsens women's experience of menopause and can even worsen the symptoms experienced.

As we've learned, women working through menopause are a new and growing phenomenon for organizations. However, our silence around menopause means that until now women have stepped back, or stepped away from work without anyone noticing what was going on for them. We might say that menopause has not registered as an issue before, not because women were not falling by the wayside and calling for help, but because organizations simply were not listening. The evidence was there. But who was collecting it? Who was noticing the evidence and asking why? Who was taking the discussion to the board table? Who was breaking the silence and ensuring that others stopped and did something? That is changing now and the dialogue in the media, government, among business leaders and between women themselves is all calling out for someone to take notice.

Figure 4.1: Shining a light on women's issues by taking notice and overcoming the taboo.

Now you see me; now you don't

In addition to simple ignorance, there is a stigma around menopause that stops us talking about it. Partly this is due to the invisibility of older women in our culture. Ageing women are often absent from tv screens and billboards. A study in 2013 found that 82% of UK TV presenters who are over 50 were men (total male presenters, 61%).[151] Older people are excluded from all but 2% of advertisements, and when older women *do* feature they are more likely to be confined to stereotypical domestic roles.[152] A quick search for images of a 'male office worker' will throw up images of different age groups. However, when searching for 'female office worker' almost every image shows young women. Why are older women so under-represented in visual media given their meteoric rise within the workplace?

We have been too content to see older women quietly retreat into the shadows, perhaps taking up a background support role within the shadows of the main family, workplace or societal drama. It is easy to assume that women are content to quietly disappear, without asking why or challenging whether this is acceptable. Of course, far from being redundant, older women make essential contributions to society: propping up the voluntary sector, childcare and social care work. But no research has been invested in putting a figure on this and giving it the credit that is almost certainly due.[153] Nevertheless, society seems to erase women from our mental model of a 'worker' making it less likely that their needs are considered in a work context.

With this wider loss of visibility, older women could potentially internalize a sense of what they lose as they age and can suffer psychologically as a result. No longer a potential mate, no longer a mother of younger children, perhaps no longer a sense of cool, women can start to feel they have become a 'non-person' with a weak narrative of who they are now. This can profoundly impact a woman's sense of identity and self-confidence. If women are subjected to years of invisibility with little effort to help them find a new positive identity, then it is unsurprising that many menopausal women experience anxiety and depression over and above that triggered directly by hormonal changes.

If not invisible, then the alternative identity for older women is too often something negative and worthy of disgust or ridicule. 'Crazy', 'difficult' or 'old crone'. If they don't disappear quietly, then women may offend the natural order of things and find themselves labelled accordingly. This lack of positive language around older women adds to the sense of stigma. It becomes hard for women to talk about their experience of getting older as conversations about menopause are heavily loaded with the potential for unhelpful and unwanted associations. It is notable that in writing this book, the term 'older women', itself, has triggered discomfort in those reviewing the early drafts.

Associations matter. Unconsciously, society conflates being old and female with being less capable, less engaging and less confident. Even if these thoughts are not voiced, they can nevertheless become a self-fulfilling prophecy. Various research studies point towards the impact of attractiveness in men and women on perceptions of competence at work. However, they also point to the relative decline in perceived female attractiveness with ageing compared to the perceived attractiveness of older men.[154]

For women, there is a more significant cost in visible ageing where this triggers negative biases. If an older woman is not expected to perform, then she is given fewer opportunities to prove otherwise; her successes are missed; and her failure unfairly pinned on her. Research based on 40,000 job applications proved that while men in their 60s are less likely to be invited to interview than younger men, the impact of age discrimination kicks in 10 years earlier for women.[155] In fact, there is a measurable difference in interview rates for women from the age of 40 years.[156] The findings are confirmed in other studies on job hiring processes, which not only show a particular bias against women as they age, but which also show that ageism increases for ethnic minorities with black British women experiencing the highest level of age discrimination.[157]

Ageism is an invisible barrier that both men and women encounter at work. However, the power of its impact is far greater for women both in terms of its earlier onset due to menopause and the more negative associations that ageing has for women. Our cultural prejudices against older women make it hard for us to engage with menopause and to discuss its impact dispassionately. Meanwhile, left un-named, this prejudice has the power to significantly worsen outcomes for women, with older women finding themselves victimized. Qualitative research identified a range of themes that result: threats to feelings of competence; self-doubt and helplessness; being subjected to 'momism'; feeling isolated and lonely; and gradual disengagement from the workplace.[158]

There are signs things are changing for the better. More positive narratives are emerging for older women. These need to be restated again and again, if not shouted from the rooftops. With a more positive focus women can find their post-menopausal years full of meaning, purpose, wisdom, adventure, fun, and with continued personal growth and unfettered achievement. Many see the ending of periods and the risk of pregnancy as something to genuinely celebrate. Some have taken to calling this stage 'menostart' versus 'menopause'[159] and others urge women to reclaim their power as they experience menopause,[160] shaping a positive narrative of their own in order to come out the other side smiling. We need to hear of, and see, the role models that prove this is more than simply rhetoric.

Figure 4.2: Women need positive role models who celebrate the strengths and potential of women experiencing menopause.

No more 'Keeping mum' about women's bodies

On top of ignorance and stigma, there can be feelings of embarrassment and shame in discussing physical symptoms. Mentioning problems with excessive or chaotic bleeding is likely to trigger a sense of disgust.[161] If the problem is too little blood we can evoke feelings of pity, or horror, for a woman's apparent lost fertility. While women might be brave enough to discuss some symptoms and the impact these are having, they might continue to ringfence discussion of other debilitating issues. Nobody is likely to start discussing vaginal dryness with their line manager even though this could be a significant cause of pain and stress. Even outside of work, women may find it difficult to disclose what they are going through with partners or their closest friends. 'Keeping mum', or maintaining secrecy, about physical symptoms adds to a profound sense of isolation for many women experiencing menopause. This is stronger still within cultures where the taboo around women's bodies is more powerful.

While there may be embarrassment in mentioning physical symptoms, it can also be risky to bring up emotional or psychological symptoms that could raise doubts about a woman's capability and resilience. As is the case for mental health conditions, there can be difficulties in raising awareness of cognitive and emotional challenges in a work context given the general stigma around mental illness.[162] However, more than for men, women can find their mental health challenges are put down to their own longer-term fragility and their inherent make-up, rather than being seen as an understandable response to the situation they find themselves in. This makes it additionally risky for a woman to raise in a work context.

When women need time off for their menopause symptoms, they are more likely to keep the reasons to themselves. The CIPD study showed, that women often worried about disclosing their menopause symptoms in case others would presume their performance to be affected. Very often they believed their manager would not be supportive. In the Fawcett Society research, 26% of women who were working during the menopause transition had taken time off due to symptoms at some point. However, only 30% of these had specified menopause on their sick note. Most simply stated the symptom itself, such as anxiety or depression. Keeping menopause symptoms secret led to women experiencing higher levels of stress and often a worse impact on their work as a result.

Women's readiness to disclose menopause is likely to be impacted by whether they see and hear it being treated with respect. Sadly, in the Fawcett Society report, 1 in 5 of those working during menopause saw it being treated as a joke. Humour can be a helpful outlet for difficult experiences and can encourage openness. However, if women become aware of a culture that is hostile towards them, perhaps where menopause is treated as a subject of ridicule, this can significantly undermine a woman's confidence and trigger worse performance.[163]

Figure 4.3: Menopause humour can feel demeaning and undermine women's confidence.

No one should feel a pressure to disclose personal or medical information, and perhaps it is unnecessary to broadcast to everyone the full gory details. Nevertheless, if the reality of menopause remains wrapped up in a knowing wink or vague phrases such as 'women's troubles', or 'going through the change';

it can be very hard to understand an individual's specific needs. The more we normalize conversations about menopause symptoms and how these vary from person to person, the easier it gets to lift the veil and to respond with appropriate empathy and practical support.

Just a bit hormonal?

Nobody would be surprised to discover that women's bodies are different from men's, yet in a work context this fact has the potential to trigger controversy because 'different' has too often been taken as meaning 'lesser', and the word 'hormonal' too often taken to mean irrational, unreliable and unsuited to work. There is a silence around the potential impact of hormones that does not only come from men. There are a lot of women who deeply fear triggering unwelcome stereotypes.

What can come as a surprise, even among medical experts, is that differences go beyond reproductive organs, muscle strength and the presence or absence of chest hair. Medicine is only now acknowledging that basing medical science on the male body alone may not be serving women that well.[164] It is astounding that the first ever anatomy training model based on a woman's body was created in 2022, meaning that until now trainee doctors were unfamiliar with female bone structure, organ sizes or indeed the position and orientation of a uterus. When considering women's bodies in the past, 'difference' was transmuted into a sense of 'lesser', with male bodies as the ideal and women's as woefully flawed versions that could be safely discounted. Now, as our understanding develops around women and, specifically, around menopause, we are starting to explore more fully the differences between men and women, but at the same time challenge the concept of women's bodies being inherently wrong relative to a man's.

A key difference between men's and women's bodies is the monthly fluctuation in hormone levels that women experience through the menstrual cycle. These fluctuations can become more dramatic and debilitating in the run-up to menopause. Although the hormonal cycle is intrinsic to the magic of how a woman functions, discussing the impact of hormones on women at work challenges an area of taboo. Women have fought for generations to be taken seriously and to have their potential and value recognized. Women have battled against unfair biases and prejudices that assume they cannot perform as effectively and consistently as a man. In this context, 'being a bit hormonal' is the ultimate put down for a woman, and admitting to the power of hormones, the ultimate betrayal of women's road to equality.

The truth is, women can and do succeed at the highest levels in all walks of life – including academia, government, business and sport. However, that does not mean they achieve this without ever experiencing cyclical changes in mood, focus, physical strength and confidence.[165] They succeed despite such cyclical changes. Indeed, they may achieve super-resilience directly because of the strategies they must adopt to sustain performance. Research in education often finds differences between genders in the conditions that contribute to success.[166] There was a time where it was assumed girls were academically inferior to boys, and yet with changes to teaching approaches such as an increase in coursework versus exams, and with growing opportunities, girls regularly outperform boys. The same principles apply to a work context. If women and men equally deserve a place within an organization, then practices need to change so that both can perform and thrive equally well.

In denying the power of hormones, we have tacitly encouraged the world to carry on working only with the model male body. Where medicine failed to develop the right diagnoses, operating tools and drug doses to treat women's bodies, organizations have failed to develop the right design and practices to help women perform at their best. By recognizing that men and women might have differences that impact how they succeed at work, we must be careful not to paint a picture that women are flawed due to their hormones and are destined to struggle in an organizational environment. This does women a great disservice. However, the opposite is also true. Asserting that hormones have no impact on women at all is potentially just as harmful as it negates the reality many women experience and with which they must contend to succeed. As our approach to equality has matured to one of equity and authenticity it is essential that we tactfully revisit and explore any differences that impact not only the making of babies but also women's relationship to work.

The problem ain't women!

As we have heard, older women may experience difficulties with work, and in part this is due to menopause. However, this does not mean that older women are designed wrong for work. It is rather a strong sign that work needs to be redesigned with older women in mind. The relationship between menopause symptoms and work is bi-directional.[167] It is often the interaction between a woman's experience of menopause and the work environment that can serve to trigger or exacerbate negative experiences of menopause.

The clue is in the queue

In many respects we still live in a man's world, albeit one where there may be the occasional nod to women's different needs. Public toilets are a case in point. Putting aside the challenges in catering appropriately for the trans and non-binary community, think about the difference in queue length between men's and women's toilets. Anyone who's been to a major sporting event or concert, or even their local pub, will be only too familiar with this.

Figure 4.4: The world is not always designed with women's needs in mind; queues for the female toilet are a visible sign.

There are various interpretations of this issue. Some relate to attribution bias – a tendency to blame issues on the person when that person is not one of us:

- ▶ Women go to the toilet too often. Their bladder control must be poor.
- ▶ Women stay in the toilet too long. They must wear over-complicated clothing.
- ▶ Women spend too long queuing. They must spend too much time chatting with others.

Some interpretations relate to apathy – accepting how things are:

- ▶ We don't have enough toilets for women. Oh well, it must suck to be a woman.
- ▶ Women are used to queuing for the toilet. They'll deal with it.
- ▶ Women could always leave the show 10 minutes before the interval starts if they don't want to queue.

The over-riding interpretation is one where the male-centric view is taken as the ideal or the norm from which women deviate or fall short:

- ▶ Men are better designed for toilet-going. They can stand up and use urinals.
- ▶ Men are quicker. They are more efficient.
- ▶ Men don't complain about toilets. They are easier to deal with.

The problem never gets solved because, firstly, building designers do not care sufficiently that women are having a poorer experience and, secondly, they are not prepared to invest in designing spaces with women in mind. Designers may know how much toilet space is needed for women to achieve an equitable provision (equitable provision would mean that women can use the toilets without having to queue for any longer than men). But in practice, it's easier to simply block out 20m2 on this side for the men and 20m2 on that side for the women. Job done. It's possible, however, that building designers really don't know. With so many aspects of our world, as exposed by Caroline Perez in her book *Invisible Women*, a significant data gap exists that would enable us to ensure equitable outcomes.[168]

If we extrapolate the toilet problem to all aspects of how we designed work, we can see how we might start to confuse women's difficulty in navigating work as a problem with the women, rather than as a sign that work has not been designed right. Work can demand particular hours and locations; certain rules for proving your worth; that everyone must wear a particular type of uniform or comply with the same strict rest times. The expectations have evolved on the assumption that a good worker is one who works like a younger person or a man and who can keep any alternative needs hidden.[169]

More than an inconvenience, poor work design for women experiencing menopause can result in actual harm. The British

Occupational Hygiene Society (BOHS) issued a joint report in 2022 emphasizing the disproportionate burden carried by women in terms of occupational disease[170] as a result of the physical demands and risks women are exposed to. For women working through menopause who are in manual professions or working on their feet, there can be a higher risk of joint pain and fatigue.

Do we just need more fans?

Of course, when we move beyond toilets to thinking about whole organizations, things get a lot more complex. Increasingly, organizations are adopting a systems-thinking approach to ensure they are able to create meaningful change.[171] Unfortunately, when we seek to understand the world around us, too often we still use a 'linear' scientific approach to look for patterns of cause and effect and fail to see the solution lies beyond more toilets, or as is often the case with menopause, an order for extra desk fans!

Figure 4.5: Menopause actions need to offer far more than extra desk fans.

Our attraction to simplicity can mask the true messiness of complex problems and stops us holding and appreciating that full complexity. As a result, we can end up with a fragmented collection of solutions that do not necessarily deliver the total combined outcome we require.[172] In the early days of management science, Frederick Taylor and others such as Lillian and Frank Gilbreth transformed how industrial processes were refined by using science to discover how to minimize the waste of time and resources and optimize process efficiency.[173] By breaking industrial processes down and systematically experimenting with different constituent elements, Taylor was able to refine the end-to-end process and reduce variability in efficiency, productivity and quality. Taylorism still influences how we understand and manage organizations today. However, critics have also recognized from early on the limitations of observing organizations through a singular mechanistic or reductionist lens and have expanded the approach to take a broader 'systems thinking' view.

We now recognize that while we can learn a great deal by isolating particular elements in an organizational process, this can also overlook the inherent complexity of the whole system – especially where the system incorporates people. It is risky to assume that by manipulating one variable, as one would in a scientific laboratory, you can get a simple predictable outcome; rather, one needs to try to understand all the interconnecting elements and their relationships to one another to anticipate fully how the overall system will respond to a change. Although Taylor achieved efficiencies, the refinement of industrial processes also had a negative impact for the people who operated them over the long-term. There was a strong backlash from many quarters over Taylor's apparent treatment of people as if they were extensions of the machines.[174]

How Taylorism doesn't always add up

Previously workers might use their skill and craftsmanship to create products, with variable standards of outcome. Taylor, therefore, designed mechanistic processes where people required less individually developed capability. By following clearly laid-out steps and rules, using scientifically designed machinery and production processes, workers could create more predictable high-quality and efficient results.

The difficulty is that changes to the mechanistic elements also impacted the people who operated them. By subjugating skilled labourers to automatons that simply execute standard operating procedures, Taylor to some extent overlooked workers' psychological and emotional needs. No longer could workers derive the same level of pride and satisfaction from exercising their skill, autonomy and creativity; planning of tasks was separated out to be done by management.

Taylor did recognize the need for trust and friendship between workers in order to maintain their performance. However, principally he assumed that workers would always do the minimum required and that they would only work hard if productivity was rewarded through 'piece rate' pay. He also assumed that due to the lower skill requirement workers would be cheaper and easier to replace. However, workers' motivation and performance are not so easily manipulated as this assumes. Even with higher remuneration, workers can still become bored, dissatisfied and eventually leave. Even low-skilled workers will be more motivated and committed to stay where they can learn and grow and exercise some level of autonomy and control.

> If people repeatedly get bored and leave, this raises hiring and training costs. Furthermore, there would be greater levels of industrial action and discord. So, by focusing purely on the efficiency of processes, Taylor risked undermining the sustainability and cost-efficiency of the system as a whole.

Since the 1930s, we have seen psychological science divert interest increasingly towards the people within the process and the importance of understanding individuality and personality when designing sustainable systems. As well as matching processes to people's physical needs, we also take into account the psychological needs that help people to work at their optimum, such as their need for meaning, control, mastery and rewarding relationships.[175,176] By studying all these 'human factors' we can design better tools and processes that are matched to the possibilities and limitations of human physiology, cognition and emotion. These principles have been applied in many settings.

A powerful example of the application of systems-thinking is within the aviation industry where it is used to optimize safety and performance. This can be partly informed by studying each element within the system; the aircraft, the communications, the people. Critically, however, it depends on understanding how the different elements in the system interact and work together as a whole. In the early days of aviation, the focus was on finding pilots with the right characteristics to fit the demands of the aircraft. This uses a Tayloristic approach of designing an efficient machine and assuming people would fit with that. However, as aircraft became more complex there was more recognition that the matching of human and machine was a two-way street. Our understanding of what people could, or couldn't, typically do informed the way in which aircraft structures and controls were designed. Indeed, rather than just being about the human–machine interaction, it also required an understanding of the interaction between different crew members and how they worked in partnership. More than that, ergonomics methodologies have moved from focusing on individual tasks in aviation to 'entire systems, the constraints shaping behaviour and the culture of organizations'.[177]

Sometimes the impact of these inter-relationships is hard to predict but become evident when something goes wrong and there is an accident. An air accident analysis cannot explain cause and effect by either looking at machine or human factors alone; but must consider these in tandem. It requires a multi-dimensional, systems thinking, approach to understand how the machine's design, maintenance, crew, and training contributed collectively to the outcome. It also takes a multi-dimensional, systems thinking, approach to identify how to avoid a similar accident happening again.

Case study: Air accident

In 1989, a Boeing 737 crashed on an embankment of the M1 motorway near Kegworth, UK, leading to the deaths of 47 passengers from the 126 people on board. The accident analysis showed a complex web of relationships between aircraft maintenance, aircraft design, display design, human perception and decision-making processes, training and experience, organizational culture, communication between cabin and flight deck, and simple unfortunate coincidence. The survivability of the accident was also affected by features such as safety belt design, passenger seat design, cabin storage design and the structural integrity of the cabin floor.[178] To ensure the events and their consequences would not be repeated would similarly take a multi-dimensional systems-wide approach. Recommendations were made looking at all these elements and their interactions.

Applying systems-thinking to menopause

For women experiencing menopause, we must explore the interconnections within the working environment, the social and cultural environment, and the context of a woman's broader life experience at the time. Making organizations more menopause friendly does not mean just adding in a training session, or a flexible work policy, a shipment of extra desk fans or, for that matter, extra toilets. Simply adding things in may not alter the fact that the system still favours younger people and men. To offer meaningful support for menopause, we need to take a more strategic approach and look at how all elements of organizational design fit with what older women need. This includes considering interacting elements that define where people work, when they work, how work is structured, evaluated and rewarded, and how people interact.

Systems thinking also encourages us to look beyond the connections within a current system. Systems also evolve in response to changing external forces and pressures. Organizational systems of today now exist in a very different context from even 10 years ago. The need for society to ensure that women can stay economically active for longer alongside the societal changes that exacerbate the pressures experienced by women at this time mean that new organizational systems are needed.

Achieving such systemic change goes beyond the scope of a single diversity champion or indeed the whole HR department. It requires a more strategic approach that crosses the whole organizational landscape and requires engagement from everyone who designs and implements each element of how the organizations operates. All of this requires sponsorship from the very top to inspire, spearhead and underwrite the wide range of actions that are involved in fulfilling their commitment to being menopause friendly.[179]

Empowerment lost and found

Great organizational design takes account of what will attract, engage, develop, and retain people over the long term. It has been proven that people do best and stick around when they feel empowered at work.[180,181] However, women who work through menopause can too often lose their sense of empowerment with consequences for their performance and motivation at work.

Position in full sun

Until now the onus has largely been on women to do all the work of adapting to the organizational environment; managing, or simply hiding, symptoms in order to get on at work. Like a flower planted in the shade, she might make a reasonable show of adapting; establishing roots and producing shoots through the power of her own resilience. However, it is only when the environment gives the right enrichment that she is able to fully bloom.

Evidence shows that women can adapt to menopause partly through adopting a positive mindset.[182] This is a skill that can be developed via CBT with benefits for health and well-being.[183] However, positive thinking only succeeds up to a point. When women mask what they are dealing with and try simply to cope, the burden of holding work, home and health in balance can make it extremely difficult for them to maintain their motivation and thrive.

Helping women find psychological strategies to cope, must work hand in hand with consideration of how the working environment contributes to optimum empowerment. A woman cannot single-handedly decide to feel empowered, while simultaneously feeling that this is being threatened by her work. Empowerment is not only a personal quality but a by-product of context and relationships.[184] There is good empirical evidence for looking at empowerment through such multiple lenses.[185] Where line managers do not create the right environment that supports empowerment, we see an increase in employee turnover.[186] For example, a key measure of empowerment is how confident employees are to speak up when they see a problem. But for this to happen, the ground must first be laid by leaders so that employees feel able to 'break the silence'[187] on workplace issues.

Various aspects of organizational design can undermine empowerment, such as work overload, role conflict, and job insecurity. Meanwhile, transactional and toxic leadership can further undermine an employee's need for autonomy, relatedness and competence.[188] It is vital to turn the light up on individual needs to optimize motivation. Line managers play a critical intermediary role, especially for staff who do not already have the knowledge and experience to exercise autonomy.[189] Unfortunately, very often leaders lack awareness of the actions they, themselves, can take that positively impact employee empowerment.[190]

Restoring empowerment

There are various models of empowerment that help us to understand what women working through menopause might need to help them participate, perform, progress and thrive.

- ▶ Deci and Ryan outline three core factors in human motivation within their Self Determination Theory (SDT): autonomy, competence and relatedness.[191] For menopausal women all three of these can become significantly eroded, resulting in a loss of psychological empowerment. At the same time all three can be restored through a combination of supporting a change in mindset, and also through creating changes to the working culture and environment.[192] SDT has been demonstrated to be a good theoretical foundation for coaching practice[193] and working with individual women.

> Spreitzer's mode of empowerment incorporates a similar three factors but adds a fourth, 'meaning', to reflect the importance of alignment between person's values and beliefs and the organization where they work.[194]

> Hickey et al. look at a medical model for empowerment of women through menopause. They combine elements of informed and shared decision-making, the need to challenge stigma, the creation of menopause-friendly work environments and the importance of supportive relationships.[195,196]

Looking at the core elements of these models we can see how menopause can negatively impact empowerment but also where there is scope for positive action to restore empowerment. Research has shown how coaching working women through menopause can have positive benefits for their empowerment with material improvements in health and well-being.[197] Similarly, empowerment-based approaches within a clinical setting have improved outcomes for women receiving health counselling and fitness coaching around menopause;[198,199,200] and for people with disabilities.[201] Even so, women often find it difficult to overcome stigma and to use coaching opportunities as a platform for discussing their menopause experiences.[202]

Any empowerment approach must be led by what women want rather than being based on assumptions. One study directly asked what women wanted from their managers in relation to support on menopause. The emerging themes highlighted the importance of manager knowledge and awareness; manager communication skills and behaviour; but also, employer actions such as staff training, and supportive integrated staff policies.[203]

Bringing all this together, we can conclude that empowering women through menopause comes down to five core factors:

1. Meaning or purpose
2. Knowledge and insight for informed decision-making
3. Autonomy, or control
4. Competence, or effectiveness
5. Relatedness

These are all explored more fully in the text that follows.

Meaning or purpose

As women experience the menopause transition, they can find that their identity, needs and ambitions diverge from those of the organizations where they work. This has the potential to increase the strain experienced by women and erode their resilience.[204] Where organizations see the value in keeping women engaged through menopause there is the potential to reconnect with women and establish a renewed shared purpose.

Knowledge and insight for informed decision-making

The lack of knowledge and awareness around menopause has significantly limited women's ability to speak up and name their needs, or for organizations to identify potential solutions. By addressing taboo and working to fill the knowledge gap, organizations can lay the foundations for valuable conversations where women feel understood and heard, and where they can find ways to maximize their impact at work.

Autonomy, or control

A working woman's autonomy or sense of control can be compromised as she experiences menopause, damaging her motivation and optimism. The inevitability of menopause, along with the lottery of symptoms a woman may or may not experience, can contribute to a feeling of powerlessness. The remedy for this is to boost women's ability to choose what happens within the workplace. However, very often the work environment offers few options to ease the pressure, or it assumes a one-size-fits-all approach to menopause.

It is critical, at this stage, that women are given as much opportunity as possible to exercise choice in the medical or non-medical treatment they receive, and also in how they balance the management of symptoms alongside continuing to work. This means women need to be given options for dealing with the pressures, where they can have a meaningful influence on the demands they face. They need a good awareness of these options and support in making informed choices. Importantly, they need to know they can shape a solution that is right for them as an individual. This means they need to be given a voice and be listened to as experts in their life situation.

Competence or effectiveness

Many women see menopause symptoms having a detrimental impact at work and incur an increasing personal cost in trying to maintain their level of performance. Although striving even harder than before to deliver, performance can nevertheless falter, resulting in criticism or harsh treatment from colleagues. All of this serves to undermine a woman's confidence in her capability and her longer-term potential to succeed.

A compassionate approach can help a woman to adapt and grow so she is able to right herself in the face of change. With support, women can find strategies to make the best use of their enduring strengths. With investment in their development, they can re-learn how to perform within the context of their changing bodies.

Growing confidence can also mean women standing up and advocating for themselves. It is ok for a woman to call out when an employer neglects to provide the environment she needs to thrive. It is ok for a woman to ask for the adjustments that restore her ability to perform.

Relatedness

Women experiencing menopause can feel a much greater sense of 'otherness' at work and lose the positive connections that contribute to their overall job satisfaction and well-being. The pressure to keep menopause hidden from colleagues can lead to women struggling to cope alone. This can directly worsen symptoms and their impact of symptoms. Even where a woman is managing ok, the stigma around menopause can make it hard to authentically connect with colleagues who have not faced similar challenges. Stigma can also get in the way of women making connections with other women who are also experiencing menopause and who may provide important allyship. Furthermore, where working environments are particularly toxic, disparaging comments and inappropriate humour can harm women's self-esteem and inner confidence.

A sense of belonging and connectedness, is known to be fundamental to human health and motivation, and to an individual's personal power.[205] Strengthening the availability of multiple supportive relationships at work is key.

With a clearer understanding of the barriers to women working through menopause, we can move towards meaningful action. Action starts by addressing the silence that can persist around menopause. However, deeper change requires a strategic and systemic approach. It is not for women to do all the work of challenging the status quo or adapting their mindset. We need to ensure that workplaces are set up to enable women to better perform and thrive.

Key themes in Chapter 4

1. Our ignorance on menopause has prevented us from recognizing the issues and taking action within organizations.

2. The taboo around menopause and ageing in women stops people speaking up and finding solutions.

3. Women can learn strategies to adapt to the challenges, using a more positive mindset alongside an honest evaluation of their changing needs.

4. Organizations must also provide an empowering environment that enables women to succeed given their real-life challenges.

5. Change means challenging how organizations do things, with menopause in mind.

6. Meaningful change requires a wide range of integrated systemic actions.

7. The best action plans will consider menopause from a biopsychosocial perspective; understanding that positive change is not only achieved through a woman's access to medical and lifestyle support but also through a combination of psychological, social, and physical environment changes in the workplace.

PART 2
FROM AWARENESS TO ACTION

5
M-POWERED: a framework for creating a menopause action plan

Building on an understanding of the physical, psychological, social and environmental factors impacting women as they work through menopause, and an appreciation of the processes that support organizational change, Brew People has developed the M-POWERED framework to help structure and direct an organization's menopause action plan.

The M-POWERED framework can be used as a foundation for auditing what your organization already is doing to be more menopause-friendly and for monitoring impact over the longer term as you enhance these actions. It positions your menopause action plan in a strategic context and highlights the importance of ensuring changes are integrated across organizational systems.

Actions address what can be done at an organizational, leadership, team and individual level to enable women to participate, perform, progress and thrive whilst working through menopause.

Table 5.1: M-POWERED framework explained

M:	Menopause		A *menopause* action plan creates the following:
P	Purpose		Stakeholders engaged in a shared *purpose*
O	Openness		Courage and *openness* to talk and to learn
W	Will		Personal *will* and agency, in voice and choice
E	Effectiveness		Ability, potential, and *effectiveness*
R	Relationships		Supportive, trusting *relationships*, and culture
E	Environment		Menopause-friendly physical *environment*
D	Delivery		Sustainable and systemic *delivery*

These actions are supported by detailed guidance on key questions to address as an employer, and ways to lead individual conversations on menopause. Each element of the framework is backed up by case study examples to illustrate how others already are implementing these in practice.

6
Purpose: stakeholders engaged in a shared *purpose*

You may struggle to get a menopause action plan off the ground at all if you cannot articulate its purpose to others and secure their backing. Key stakeholders in your organization will ask:

- Why do we need to do anything?
- What difference will it make if we take action?
- What's the return on investment (ROI) if we invest time and money on this?

This is not simply a top-down exercise. There must be a clear alignment between the organization's aims and women's own drivers. A clearly aligned purpose will help you to put your money where it really matters and achieve the maximum return. Consultation is key to shaping your purpose and engaging stakeholders along the way.

The purpose may be unique to your organization. To secure support for systemic change, it's fundamental to articulate the commitments you are making and what this will deliver in terms of social impact or the commercial benefits.

In this chapter, I provide a guide for engaging stakeholders behind a shared purpose on menopause, illustrated with case studies. I offer tools for developing a compelling business case, estimating ROI, planning a communicating strategy.

Demonstrate strategic alignment

Your first task is to present the business case for a menopause-friendly strategy in the light of your organization's own priorities and constraints. Personalizing your action plan will ensure your key stakeholders are all fully on board and inspired to lead and support your organization on this journey. You might be able to sign off on the odd bit of awareness training without senior executive involvement. However, if you want to work more systemically then you will need to secure top-down investment of cash, time, leadership input and resources. This means turning your menopause ambitions into the language that senior stakeholders understand and fully articulating the return on investment in being menopause friendly.

Becoming more menopause friendly can be an aim in itself, and a way of expressing the organization's egalitarian values. However, it can also be a vehicle that helps the organization achieve its commercial vision and financial goals. Review your mission and the concerns of key stakeholders. What are the key areas where you feel being menopause friendly could make a difference to the organization and where the interests of the different stakeholder groups, including women themselves, could align?

What are the personal drivers for the women who work with you?

- Increasing *participation* at work through sustaining longer hours or full-time working?
- Improving *performance* and build confidence in capability and future potential?
- Enabling *progression* by removing barriers to development or promotion?
- *Thriving* at work, with better work–life balance and inclusion?

What are your organization's strategic drivers around menopause?

- Enabling *growth* through the attraction and retention of a wider diversity of valuable talent?
- Improving *organizational* performance by improving the diversity of senior leadership and by optimizing female talent?

- ▶ Improving *productivity* by improving individual participation, effectiveness and by reducing sickness absence?

- ▶ Improving *sales and service* delivery through improved alignment with older female customers and service users?

- ▶ Improving *shareholder value* through building and preserving a positive values-led brand?

- ▶ Meeting *social obligations and commitments* to employee well-being and equity?

- ▶ Delivering higher *social return on investment* by considering the organization's wider role in society?

- ▶ Consider the synergies between women's personal drivers and your organization's strategic drivers.

Case study: Virgin Media O2

For some years, Virgin Media O2 has taken action to break the taboo around menopause and to foster open dialogue. They were the first telecommunications company to achieve the Henpicked 'Menopause-Friendly Employer' accreditation. More recently, through listening to the diverse views of employees, it was clear there was a need to move beyond creating openness and to adopt a more structured approach to menopause actions within the context of a clearer strategic purpose. In their 2024 Pay Gap Report, Virgin Media O2 cite being Menopause Friendly as a key intervention for closing the gender pay gap,[206] demonstrating just one area where menopause

> actions can impact business outcomes. By implementing the BSI Standard for 'menstruation, menstrual health and menopause in the workplace' they have also been able to embed menopause actions with an even clearer communication of the business case.[207]

For some organizations or sectors the role played by older women is critical, meaning there is additional utility in aligning the organization's and women's aims. For example, the healthcare sector relies on a predominantly female workforce but can struggle with recruitment and retention. In fact, since Covid there are acute challenges in the healthcare sector with older women stepping away from employment. Therefore, there is much to gain by investing in menopause policies and actions right now.

For other organizations, there may be a lack of female representation in key roles and senior levels. This could have consequences for decision making, customer connection, and gender pay gap. It might simply be limiting your ability to secure the best talent or fuel growth. Here, a menopause action plan could be critical to increasing the diversity of the organization, through broadening your talent pool.

On the other hand, a menopause-friendly culture may be a vital way to demonstrate your organization's values and social commitments.

> ### Case study: NHS, North East and North Cumbria
>
> With a predominantly female workforce (77%), around a fifth of NHS employees are within a typical menopause age range. Taking action on menopause is

vitally important to the well-being and performance of staff but also ensures that levels of patient care are sustained. Within the North East and North Cumbria region of the NHS, menopause actions are additionally framed within the context of the organization's wider societal impact. Within the UK, the region has the highest rate of deaths by suicide with the highest rates among women aged 45–49 years. In 2024 the organization piloted a non-prescribing menopause clinic for staff. This gave women time to discuss their symptoms and the impact these had on them at work. It also empowered women to make informed decisions and create strategies for advocating their healthcare needs and addressing workplace challenges.[208]

What might further increase the value of a menopause action plan in your organization?

- ▶ Does your organization or sector depend on a predominantly female workforce?
- ▶ Is it particularly important for your organization to retain all those with knowledge and experience?
- ▶ Is your organization being held back by an overly narrow talent pool?
- ▶ Is it critical that your organization sets an example or is seen to deliver social impact via its actions on menopause?

Estimate the return on investment

Philosophically, business leaders might appreciate the many ways in which it is helpful for an organization to be more menopause friendly. But it's far more powerful if you can put some numbers to it.

Being menopause friendly will save your organization money. It is estimated, that on average it costs approximately £30,000 to replace a member of staff, assuming an average salary of £25,000[209] – much more if it is for a senior role. What is staff attrition around menopause costing you?

As explored in Chapter 3, there are financial and reputational penalties if an organization falls short of accepted standards around menopause. If an organization competes on the strength of attracting the best talented workforce or through maintaining a strong ethical stance, it is essential this brand image is preserved. Marketing departments will, no doubt, put a value to this brand. Where brand reputation is damaged, what would you estimate to be the value that is potentially lost?

At the same time there are significant commercial benefits in taking action. A menopause action plan could enable your organization to differentiate itself in the market, grow market share and improve productivity all of which deliver value in cold hard cash. Can you put a figure to the benefits that a menopause action plan will deliver?

What is the pay-back or the potential costs for your organization?

▶ What benefits of being more menopause friendly can you identify: for employees; for customers and service users; and for the organization as a whole?

▶ What value can you attach to the benefits?

▶ What are the potential costs of inaction?

Evaluating the commercial returns can help to prioritize investment in menopause-friendly actions. Initially, you may need to experiment and track progress on a few quick wins. Research on the effectiveness of different interventions is still developing. However, learning from other pioneer organizations can be invaluable to hear what has already been tried and tested in practice and where you might focus attention first.

How might you demonstrate ROI in your organization?

- What budget do you require for the range of actions needed?
- What is the anticipated impact of these actions?
- What investments might be needed in the short, medium and longer-term?
- What are the quick wins or priority actions?
- How can you track ROI to learn and build on the experience you gain?

Engage stakeholders in your menopause policy commitments

There will be a wide spectrum of people who have a vested interest in what your organization does around menopause: women already experiencing menopause, women who have that ahead of them, colleagues, line managers, HR specialists and senior leadership. A menopause action plan needs this community on board. They are the ones that will own it, drive it and embody it. It's not down to women themselves to resolve issues with flexible working policies; to challenge every instance of inappropriate ageist humour; or to fight any resistance to change among those who just don't 'get it'. The changes that will be made will involve everyone across the whole organization.

Consulting this community early is key to their engagement and the views of women, themselves, is critical. Who better to identify what would be helpful or unhelpful going forward? But, other perspectives matter too. There are practical realities to be considered in ensuring that fairness is maintained for all staff and that the whole organization's needs are supported. Through effective consultation, whether that's in groups, one-to-ones or via surveys, you will be able to do a better job of working out what action plan will energize the community as a whole and result in the most effective change.

> **What is needed to engage a change community in your organization?**
>
> ▶ Who will need to be part of any community action on menopause?
>
> ▶ What is their current knowledge or attitude to menopause?
>
> ▶ How ready are they to play their part?
>
> ▶ What questions and concerns might they have that will need to be answered?
>
> ▶ What opportunities can you create to consult with stakeholders and explore how best to engage them?

Support is strongest where you have engaged your target community well ahead of making any firm public commitments. However, there comes a point when it pays to publish your menopause manifesto and everything that is going to happen to make this a reality. In doing so, you will make clear what role others must play for the promises around menopause to be met. You also make clear that the organization can be held accountable for upholding its menopause commitments.

A well-written menopause policy goes a long way to addressing the risk of legal action. More importantly, it sends an important signal that being menopause friendly matters. It clarifies the scope of ambition and the standard the organization wants to achieve. It spells out what actions will be taken, who will be responsible, and when these will be delivered. It clarifies the resources available to support implementation and any process through which employees can call upon support in implementing the policy. Publishing a formal policy may not feel like the right approach for your organization. Even so, it pays to communicate your organization's commitment and expectations on menopause in a way that still engages others in a shared purpose and where it is clear what role others are expected to play.

What will be your organization's policy commitment on menopause? Does it communicate the following?

- ▶ The purpose of your menopause policy.
- ▶ The objectives and actions you are committing to.
- ▶ Who will share responsibility for any actions involved.
- ▶ The rules or processes people will need to comply with.
- ▶ The resources or support in place to help deliver the policy.

It doesn't stop there. More important than the policy itself is how you bring it to life. Communication, training and feedback all play a vital role in keeping the conversation going and ensuring the policy doesn't simply gather dust in the HR Department's filing system.

> **How will you engage others in delivering your policy commitments on menopause?**
> - What do stakeholders need to know, think, feel, say or do to deliver your policy commitments?
> - What strategies will maximize learning or behaviour change?
> - How will you know if your audience gets it, and how will you respond if they don't?
> - How can you help the message continue to grow and spread?

Case study: BAE Systems

Voted 'Private Sector – Menopause Employer of the Year 2024', BAE Systems are four years into their journey to become menopause friendly. In a male-dominated tech sector, they place high strategic importance on attracting and retaining women. The senior level sponsorship from Sir Simon Lister, MD of BAE Systems' Naval Ships business, enabled them to go beyond simply publishing a menopause policy statement, preferring to call it their menopause 'commitment'. They have gone on to build an award-winning menopause network, engaged gender diverse champions across the business, training to help build a supportive culture, plus coaching and a menopause hub to empower individual women.[210,211]

Policies should never stand still. Menopause at work is an emerging issue, so it is even more important to keep the policy evolving through regular consultation, review and updates.

> **What provision is needed to keep your policy up to date?**
>
> ▶ How will you evaluate the effectiveness of the policy?
>
> ▶ How will you refine the commitments and actions in the face of any new insight or evidence?

Having a strong, clear purpose is a vital foundation to your menopause action plan. This will help you to engage all those responsible in delivering change and keep people on track to deliver what women and the business need.

Key actions in Chapter 6

1. Clarify the purpose, and any added value, a menopause action plan will deliver in your organization.
2. Identify how your action plan will impact women.
3. Spot synergies between what women and the organization want.
4. Spell out any return on investment for your organization.
5. Formalize your commitment via a menopause policy.
6. Develop a communication strategy to engage all stakeholders.
7. Make provisions to evaluate and update any policy and actions.

7
Openness: courage and *openness* to talk and to learn

Critical to empowerment and fundamental to any menopause action plan is breaking down the taboo around menopause and encouraging information-sharing so that everyone understands the challenges, their impact and what they can do about it. Openness is key to unlocking everything else.

Openness is about encouraging dialogue. A primary action is to tackle taboo and normalize conversations about menopause so that everyone across the organizational community feels comfortable talking about it. This makes it much easier for people to ask questions, share insights, and identify actions. It opens the way for women to share their experiences and needs, and to advocate for themselves.

Openness is also about taking an honest look at how menopause is impacting women where you work. Your challenge is to get your decision-makers to wake up to the need for action by spotlighting the problem. For this, nothing shines brighter than cold, hard data. Data will reveal differences in outcomes for women that signal inequity. Testimony from women themselves will further highlight individual experiences and identify where action may be most needed.

In this chapter, I provide a guide for creating openness around menopause. This includes guidance on how to initiate and normalize conversations about menopause, so that women feel safe to advocate for their needs. It also includes gathering data and insights to allow an honest exploration of the impact menopause has on women in your organization.

Get the conversations started

Ideally, given the right environment in your organization, women experiencing menopause will feel safe to talk about it. They will know that it is a subject that others treat with respect and compassion. They will trust that others want to listen and understand and, if needed, provide support. They will have noticed more dialogue about menopause at work, they will have seen a supportive approach adopted by leaders on the subject, they will be aware of other women speaking up and getting a positive response as a result. As a result, they may approach their manager, ally or specialist menopause coach and initiate a conversation themselves. Perhaps speaking up long before any challenges become critical.

Where a woman feels able to raise the subject herself, a colleague's reactions are important for building further trust. She will need to be met with relaxed confidence, and a non-judgmental curiosity. Managers or colleagues may worry that they do not know enough about menopause, or that they may use the wrong language and cause offence. They may be concerned about showing discomfort on a topic that could be very personal. However, such concerns diminish the more regularly menopause becomes part of conversations at work.

Where talking about menopause is new, a compassionate mindset helps to overcome any initial discomfort and fear. There is no pressure to be a ready-formed expert on menopause or, more specifically, on this woman's unique situation. All that is needed at this stage is to ask questions and truly listen to what might be creating challenges for this person. Challenges might stem from the menopause symptoms themselves, or they might relate more to how the working environment and work expectations make things difficult.

> **How will you get managers and others comfortable leading a conversation through questions such as these, and their responses?**
>
> ▶ 'Thank you for sharing this with me.'
> ▶ 'Tell me more about it so I can understand what you are experiencing.'

> - 'Are there any particularly challenging symptoms that you feel comfortable telling me about?'
> - 'In what way do you feel this might be impacting how you work?'
> - 'In what way might your work, or the working environment be creating a problem for you at this time?'

Where a woman seems comfortable, the manager might ask more searching questions to uncover specific areas of challenge and the potential consequences of this.

> **What deeper insight could managers gain if they seek answers to the following?**
>
> - 'How do you feel this impacts…
>
>   … your ability to keep working and maintaining your hours?
>
>   … your confidence in yourself and your ability to deliver?
>
>   … your scope to keep developing and progressing?
>
>   … your personal well-being?'
>
> - 'With these challenges, what would help you get the most out of work?'
> - 'What would be a good outcome for you?'

It is important to remember that not all women will feel ready to initiate a conversation about menopause and may need a prompt to get started. Possibly a manager will see that the team member is appearing more stressed, having performance issues not seen before, or showing an increase in sickness absences.

Of course, any issues with well-being, performance or absence may have nothing to do with menopause, or not have been linked to menopause in the woman's own mind. She may simply not feel comfortable discussing menopause with a colleague. Care is needed not to push any woman into disclosing her health issues, or to imply that her problems are linked to ageing, which some could take as offensive. However, where a manager does feel menopause is potentially involved, they should seek to put their colleague at her ease and offer to listen and help with whatever may be going on for her. A manager might prompt the woman to consider others to talk to, such as a specialist menopause coach, if she seems uncomfortable sharing details with them.

Useful prompts might include:

▶ 'I noticed some changes in your approach to work recently. Would it be helpful to discuss it?'

▶ 'Is there anything going on for you that it would be helpful to share, perhaps in confidence?'

▶ 'Who else are you able to share your experiences with? Could I connect to anyone else for support?'

Remembering that a woman may continue to feel uncomfortable discussing menopause with a manager or a particular colleague, your organization could actively build opportunities for women to share experiences and seek support from one another. Initially, women experiencing menopause are more likely to feel safe opening up with each other. However, in time they may build up the confidence to actively advocate for themselves with others. Actions to create dialogue should draw on women's own expressed preferences and insights.

How can your organization ensure there are others to reach out to?

- What can you do to create a menopause network where women and allies can connect?
- What meeting formats would feel safer and facilitate greater openness?
- What events and communications can you use to normalize menopause as an everyday subject in your organization?

Try asking women themselves these questions:

- 'How can I or other colleagues do a better job of supporting you?'
- 'What should others do, or not do, so that you feel safe to talk about menopause when you need to?'

Case study: Holland & Barrett

Holland & Barrett has taken a proactive, inclusive approach to menopause support as part of their broader commitment to women's health in the workplace. Through a bottom-up approach, they've listened to retail colleagues to ensure support is genuinely helpful and representative. Education and awareness initiatives aim to de-stigmatize menopause and empower employees. They offer resources like free consultations with health nurses, access to mental health first aiders, and counselling. Holland & Barrett's recognition as a Menopause Friendly and Includability Committed Employer underscores their dedication to inclusivity,

> enhancing well-being, recruitment, and diverse colleague networks across the organization.[212]

Shine a light on menopause inequity

If menopause is a new area of interest where you work, then it's likely your organization will lack data around it. Women may have been quietly leaving, stepping back or struggling without anyone noticing or spotting the signs. Systems and processes may have been put in place in the best interests of fairness, but nevertheless menopause inequity is evident when the outcomes for menopausal women are compared with other groups.

Gathering evidence of the impact menopause has in your organization will help to fuel the business case and focus on what actions could be helpful. The big question is, what are we looking for? Pragmatism is needed, otherwise the search for perfect data could simply be used as an excuse for not doing anything. As a business leader you are not looking to write a PhD thesis on the current state of things. However, you are looking to answer, as effectively as is reasonable, the core question: How menopause friendly are we?

Menopause inequity can show itself through a range of hard measurable outcomes. When we spot signs of potential problems for older women at work, we can take this as an indication that the organization is not as menopause friendly as wished. The data may not tell you how the organization can fix it. However, it will evidence any imbalance in how women experiencing menopause can participate, perform, progress and thrive at work. Taking each of these important outcomes in turn, you can pinpoint useful measures to gather data on.

What should you be looking for to spot menopause inequity?

- In all cases you would be looking to see how the outcomes change as women age. You might compare outcomes for under 40s who typically have not yet entered perimenopause; 40–50 year-olds who typically will be experiencing perimenopause; and over 50s who are more likely to be post-menopausal.
- You would also, of course, be comparing the data with how men's outcomes change across the same equivalent age brackets.

Depending on your strategic priorities, where will you look for signs?

Participation:

- How do the numbers, or proportion, of women in the organization change?
- How do women's employment patterns change, e.g. full time/part time/flexible?
- When women leave where do they go, e.g. retirement/career break/self-employment/full-time role/part-time role/flexible role?

Performance:

- What changes occur in women's performance ratings?
- What changes occur in women's achievement of productivity targets?
- What changes occur in women's bonus awards?
- What common themes are observed in women's performance feedback or their development goals and how do these change?

Progression:
- How many women are applying for roles at different levels?
- What are the success rates for women in being recruited, or in gaining promotion?
- How does uptake of development opportunities change?
- What changes are observed in the gender pay gap?

Thriving:
- What changes occur in the type and level of sickness absence?
- What changes occur in incidents of accidents at work?
- What changes occur in women's uptake of occupational health support?

Listen to women and their experiences

When shaping or evaluating the impact of work practices on women, the views of women themselves are often forgotten.

These views can be invaluable to understand what is driving any inequity and also to highlight the actions that women value most. 'Listening' might include gathering ratings on questions of interest, or asking for verbatim responses. It might simply mean creating opportunities where women can talk and share their experiences.

Some data might be gathered via staff engagement surveys or exit interviews where comparisons can be made for different age groups and genders. These could give employers a general sense of how older women feel about their workplace relative to other employee groups. If the numbers are sufficient to allow any statistical modelling, it can offer insight into what might drive some of the differential outcomes seen earlier.

> **What engagement measures might it be useful to consider? For example:**
>
> ▶ Satisfaction with the role and the organization; leadership; career development opportunities; pay and recognition; culture and work environment.
>
> ▶ Readiness to work hard and support the organization's mission and values.
>
> ▶ Intention to stay long term.
>
> ▶ Pride in the organization and readiness to champion it with others.
>
> ▶ Feeling a sense of belonging with the organization.

Given the wide variation in experience, average scores can mask important issues that impact only some individual women, or which impact only small intersectional groups at work. Indeed, you may only have one woman who reports demeaning or abusive behaviour relating to menopause, but this is deeply significant to the overall question of how menopause friendly the organization is.

Qualitative data and individual case studies gathered via questionnaires, one-to-one interviews or focus groups, might enable you to hear first-hand what individual women have experienced but also to get direct input on what actions will make the greatest difference to women. Such questions can be deeply personal and therefore best asked within one-to-one discussions or where a safe group forum has been clearly established.

What opportunities can you find to explore individual women's experiences more deeply by asking questions such as these?

- 'What has been your experience of the menopause transition?'
- 'How has this impacted you at work?'
- 'What aspects of your job or working life have made it easier for you to work effectively and thrive through menopause?'
- 'What aspects of your job or working life have made it harder for you to work effectively and thrive through menopause?'
- 'What else would you like to see happen that would improve the experience for you?'
- 'What specifically can be done by: leadership; your line manager; colleagues; the wider community at work; anyone else?'

Case study: British Veterinary Association (BVA)

As part of The BVA's Good Veterinary Workplaces initiative, they took action to address the lack of awareness and confidence within the profession on addressing issues around menopause. In 2023, a sector survey found that only 14% of vets were aware of a menopause policy where they worked and that many vets would not feel confident supporting colleagues experiencing menopause. With more than half of vets

> being women, and many leaving the profession early, there is a critical need to help them stay in post and thrive. A new menopause hub provides information and resources. In addition, BVA members can access tools and coaching support via a menopause app.[213]

Encouraging openness will ensure menopause is not simply avoided or swept under the carpet in your organization. All stakeholders will benefit from an honest recognition of the challenges faced and being able to discuss these candidly with one another.

Key actions in Chapter 7

1. Provide safe opportunities for women to share more about their individual situation and needs.
2. Run regular events and communications that normalize the subject of menopause.
3. Give leaders and colleagues the skills and confidence to initiate or respond to conversations about menopause.
4. Take an honest look at how menopause is impacting women where you work.
5. Encourage discussion about what this means for your organization.
6. Learn from women themselves about their lived experience and what could help or hinder them through menopause.

7. Maintain women's right not to disclose their personal information if they choose not to and handle all information with appropriate confidentiality.

8
Will: personal *will* and agency, in voice and choice

Empowering women as they work through menopause means giving them every opportunity possible to exercise their will. This means: speaking up about their individual needs; shaping their working lives to best meet those needs; and finding solutions in partnership with their employer.

When women experience menopause symptoms that are hard to manage, in a working environment they cannot influence, and with a range of other pressures imposed on them, they can perceive a fundamental loss of autonomy, or control. They may lose their sense of personal agency and begin to see themselves more as victims of circumstance rather than able to exercise autonomy in their lives. This has significant consequences for well-being and motivation.

Strengthening this psychological empowerment depends on:

- Empowering relationships that use coaching-style interactions to facilitate women's agency, rather than dictating solutions.

- The provision of flexible options that allow women the autonomy to choose what works better for them, while also balancing this sensitively against the needs of the wider team.

- Shared responsibility for actions.

In this chapter, I provide a guide for re-igniting women's autonomy and control as they work through menopause. It includes actions for engaging women in shared decision-making and helping them request and explore the options that work best for them.

Encourage shared decision-making

Once menopause is on the table for discussion, it's time to turn the tables on the power in the discussion and open the way for women to exercise their own will and agency. It is not a time to impose solutions but to listen, show empathy, seek to understand and facilitate a collaborative discussion. It is a time when a woman should be invited to explore for herself what might be going on in her world, identify her preferred outcomes, and talk through possible actions and adjustments that could resolve it. Fundamentally, it requires a coaching interaction that allows the woman a feeling of control and choice.

> **Helpful coaching questions that encourage shared decision-making**
>
> ▶ 'What do you feel the issue is? What makes it challenging?'
>
> ▶ 'What is your perspective on what's happening for you?'
>
> ▶ 'What is important for you in the longer-term?'
>
> ▶ 'What I think I have heard you saying is… Is that right?'
>
> ▶ 'I am sorry to hear things have been difficult. Can we work out a way forward together?'
>
> ▶ 'What would you find helpful right now?'

As well as showing empathy and care, a coaching approach can also be pragmatic. It helps the woman set goals and work out what actions are needed to achieve those goals. Solutions may include practical strategies or reasonable adjustments that make working with menopause symptoms more manageable.

> **Useful questions that give back control**
>
> ▶ 'What would you like to see happen?'
>
> ▶ 'What alternative options would achieve that?'

> - 'How could we adapt this to work better for you?'
> - 'How could we help you choose the best way forward?'
> - 'What information or process might support that?'
> - 'What are your thoughts on how this could be balanced against the needs of the wider team and business?'

Empowering women to advocate for their needs gives them a greater sense of control. Paradoxically, this could also result in too much responsibility falling on the shoulders of the employer to make changes. This should not be taken as an excuse to push the problem back onto the woman to deal with herself. However, to help build confidence and a sense of ownership, managers could encourage women to take actions of their own. These questions overlap with those in Chapter 9 on Effectiveness.

> **Useful questions that encourage ownership of actions**
> - 'What actions have you tried that have helped you before?'
> - 'What other options could you explore that would enable you to sustain your current work commitments?'

Allow flexible options

To give women choice, you need to be able to put a range of flexible options on the table. Typically, these relate to where when and how people work. Without flexibility too many of your valuable female employees will choose to walk away, perhaps going to an alternative employer that does offer choice. Flexible working can bring both benefits and costs, and no single solution will be right for everyone. Helping women think this through will empower them to make more informed choices and to optimize how they work. It is also sensible to agree timeframes for reviewing how any options are working, to ensure they still meet any changing needs.

Flex the work location

Many job roles are genuinely impossible to deliver remotely, such as key roles in health and social care, teaching, factory work and cleaning. However, having the option to work from home is often popular among working women and can be particularly helpful for those experiencing menopause.

Workplace flexibility can deliver a range of benefits such as:

- Enabling women to save on travel time and have a slower start to the day when sleep is disrupted.
- Allowing women access to their private sanitary care and wash facilities.
- Minimizing anxiety that might be exacerbated by public contact and helping women to mask symptoms such as hot flushes that they can be fearful of colleagues seeing.
- Boosting productivity by minimizing distractions when experiencing cognitive symptoms.
- Giving women a greater feeling of control if they feel better placed to manage their private office space.

Workplace flexibility can, however, also have drawbacks, such as:

- Work productivity, commitment and capability being unfairly questioned. Those who are more visible can receive disproportionately more opportunities, recognition, and reward.
- Increased feelings of social isolation. This impacts women's sense of connection and belonging with the team with knock-on effects for employee well-being and organizational commitment. Over time without regular social contact, it can become harder to maintain confidence and social anxiety can increase.
- Blurred boundaries between work and home with increases in role conflict and burnout.[214]

Where possible, managers should help women think through the pros and cons of home working to achieve an ideal balance.

If an employee asks to work from home, the following questions could help them to think this through *and* help the organization work out what would be reasonable:

- 'What are the advantages of working from home for you?'
- 'What are the disadvantages of working from home for you?'
- 'What would help make this work optimally for you?'
- 'What would help make this work optimally for the team, clients, or business?'

> - 'What might you need from others to support this?'
> - 'Would you need this all the time or only at certain times?'
> - 'When could we review how any new arrangement is working for you?'

Flex the hours

Wherever work is carried out, having flexible options for the hours of work can help women achieve a balance that is effective for them. Flexing hours could mean many things such as:

- Varying start and finish times in the day depending on when best able to focus and be most productive.
- Working part-time, to enable time off to recover and rest between workdays.
- Varying non-working days depending on health needs or allowing additional paid or unpaid leave for menopause.
- Changing shift patterns. Early starts or night shifts can have a particularly detrimental impact on women suffering from sleep problems as a result of menopause.

Reducing women's participation at work through reducing their working hours can be problematic. Organizations that grant part-time working as their first option can too often lose valuable skills and labour, hampering productivity and necessitating further recruitment and training to cover the shortfall.

Women who work part time can also lose out themselves. They can see a fall in earnings and pension contributions, and often miss out on access to higher level roles where part time working may be less supported. If women work flexibly while men in your organization continue to work full time and overtime, this can become a significant contributor to your organization's gender pay gap. Organizations will need to ensure women are not pressured into making this sacrifice in the absence of efforts to make the work itself more sustainable.

Care must also be taken to differentiate regular non-working time from any time needed for menopause related sick leave or medical appointments. Depending on an employee's contractual or statutory rights, the employer may need to guard against pressuring them to use unpaid leave or non-working days for menopause-related time off.

> **If an employee asks for flexible time, the following questions could help them to think this through *and* help the organization work out what would be reasonable:**
>
> ▶ 'How could a change of hours, or working days help you?'
>
> ▶ 'Are there any negative consequences that would need to be managed for yourself or the business?'
>
> ▶ 'Do you need a regular fixed arrangement or something variable?'
>
> ▶ 'When could we review how any new arrangement is working for you?'
>
> ▶ 'If you are unable to work because of your menopause symptoms, how do our processes for recording sick leave impact you?'

Case study: Zurich

Zurich's mission is to be the most attractive employer to the widest range of people. They identified that a lack of access to flexible working options was holding people back from accessing job opportunities, particularly at more senior levels in the organization. This was contributing to a gender pay gap of around 28% in 2019. A menopause policy specifically aimed to raise awareness and confidence in discussing menopause, along with a wide range of specialist support offered to women such as access to cognitive behavioural therapy to help in the management of symptoms. Menopause actions were also integrated with a wider programme of providing access to flexible working as a default for every role. This was key to giving women at all stages in their reproductive lives the power to choose how they could work. The number of part-time female hires to a senior level more than doubled since 2019, and there was a 72% increase in applications per vacancy in the last five years – with a 110% surge in applications from females.[215,216]

Flex the deliverable

Pay gaps are particularly acute if your organization is set up to favour the 'greedy work'[217] described in Chapter 1. With a traditional monoculture of male and younger workers, high performance has tended to be equated with the following:

- ▶ Work that is delivered in a consistent way day in, day out.
- ▶ Work that is delivered in high volumes day in, day out.
- ▶ The worker being present at the office and visibly giving work their all, day in, day out.

- ▶ The worker being seen to work extra hours and readily flex to the demands of the business.

- ▶ Where workers compete for rewards and opportunities, they might regularly exceed their role expectations to stand out.

The onus is generally on workers to adapt to the employer's expectations and find a way to deliver. On the surface, this seems fair. However, this is not an equitable arrangement for women experiencing menopause who may have constraints and challenges others do not generally share.

Flexing work roles or deliverables falls outside UK legislation for flexible working as such. However, it could be a legitimate way to meet a request for reasonable adjustments, where a woman's experience of menopause symptoms constitutes a disability under UK law. There can be real benefits to the organization too. Flexing the deliverables may enable a woman to maintain her hours and overall deliver more for the organization than if she opts to go part-time. Options to consider include:

- ▶ Changing performance expectations or targets to be more achievable in the short or longer term.

- ▶ Sharing targets across a team rather than requiring each team member to deliver as clones of one another.

- ▶ Moving to a different role or adapting duties within the same role.

> **If an employee asks for adjustments to the expectations and targets of their role, the following questions could help them to think this through *and* help the organization work out what would be reasonable:**
>
> - ▶ 'What changes to your role, expectations or targets might alleviate the pressure?'

> ‣ 'What alternative deliverables could you commit to instead?'
>
> ‣ 'How could the work you deliver continue to match or complement the work of others?'
>
> ‣ 'When could we review how any new arrangement is working for you?'

> **Case study: Bank of Ireland**
>
> The Bank of Ireland's menopause policy directly addresses the challenge of providing those experiencing menopause with the flexibility they need to manage the impact of symptoms and for any medical appointments or investigations. They provide employees with up to 10 days of paid menopause leave per annum and support women who wish to avail of this by declaring any menopause-related time off work. This ensures that any absences do not impact their attendance record. With a range of other actions in place they aim to ensure women feel supported through this life stage.[218]

Know when it's ok to say 'no'

Allowing women more control and agency over how they work means finding ways to say 'yes' to requests for flexibility or reasonable adjustments. Managers should certainly not jump to saying 'no' and may have a statutory duty to explore what could work. Taking an open-minded approach and exploring how the organization could make things easier can be enough to turn the tide on the challenges being experienced. Given the wide range of flexible options, there is likely to be something your organization can offer.

Nevertheless, sometimes there will be legitimate business reason for saying 'no'. In UK law, employers can turn down a request for flexibility or other adjustment, if they deem it 'unreasonable' (see Chapter 3).

These are some of the conditions that could justify your organization turning down a request for a specific menopause action:

- Size of employer and its capacity to offer an adjustment.
- Affordability of the adjustment relative to resources available.
- Effectiveness of the adjustment at addressing any disadvantage.
- Practicality of carrying out the role with that adjustment.
- Disruption to the wider business activities.
- Health and safety risk to wider team if a change is made.
- Capability of organization to deliver the adjustment or accessibility of specialist help.

> **Think about how your organization deals with requests for flexibility or other reasonable adjustments. In what way might you need to do following?**
>
> - Set time limits on how long an adjustment will be applied.
> - Set review dates to evaluate if the action is still needed and if it is making a sufficient difference.

> Draw a line on how much flexibility you can bear as an employer, or even say 'no', if deemed appropriate.
> Seek expert legal advice.

What does everyone need to know?

> How familiar are your managers with employees' rights to request flexibility or reasonable adjustments?
> What process do you have in place to consider requests and to document this?
> What support is available for managers to explore if a request is 'reasonable'.

While some employers might be able to offer more flexibility knowing the benefits outweigh any disruption, others may be more limited. Where this happens, managers should redirect attention to where there is still some choice, or in how the available options can be adapted to better suit the employee. All the time looking to maximize a woman's freedom to exercise her will and feel some control.

Giving women some control over where, when and how they work is fundamental to empowerment. There will be limits on what your managers can agree to, but women should feel licensed to voice their needs and be supported in finding individualized solutions. Coaching questions are a powerful way to empower women in decisions that affect them.

Key actions in Chapter 8

1. Use coaching-style conversations to engage women in shared decision-making.
2. Invite individuals to express their changing needs and preferences.
3. Where possible, offer flexibility in working location, hours or deliverables.
4. Ensure managers are familiar with employees' rights for reasonable adjustments and the process for considering these.
5. Ensure managers understand where they can say no to balance individual needs with those of the wider team and organization.
6. If an option is not possible, invite the employee to explore alternatives that could work for them.
7. Highlight where managers may need expert advice and support to resolve requests for flexibility.

9
Effectiveness: ability, potential and *effectiveness*

People have an inherent desire to feel capable and confident, knowing they can effectively respond to the demands they face. They also feel more motivated when they can learn and master new skills, laying the foundations for challenges they may face in the future. When women experience menopause, their confidence often crashes. Symptoms might impact their effectiveness at work, and they can start to question their capability and potential in a way they have not done before.

Worries can become compounded by how women interpret the changes they see. They may be fearful that the challenges are permanent and will have long-term consequences. They may assume that there is no way around problems and become exhausted trying to simply mask these. They may internalize negative views of menopause and put blame on themselves.

In this chapter, I provide a guide for restoring women's confidence in their ability to deliver. It includes actions for helping women focus on their strengths but also their capacity to adapt and learn. There are suggestions for helping women challenge any unhelpful mindsets that may be holding them back.

Refocus on strengths and the capacity to adapt and grow

Women in your organization will benefit from a strengths-based approach as they experience menopause. This will enable women to re-discover themselves and through this find new confidence. Often women focus on what they have lost and how their old identity and way of working has gone. They can, however, switch their focus on who they are now and the ways in which this could deliver success and a positive impact.

> **How could your organizational practices and individual managers help women to rediscover the following?**
> - Who they are now in the light of the changes they are experiencing.
> - What energizes and motivates them now, given their new situation.
> - What matters to them in the long term and gives them purpose.
> - How their enduring or newfound strengths and qualities enable them to succeed.
> - What is going well that they can focus or build on.

While women can be supported in focusing on their strengths, their confidence mustn't be undermined by practices that fuel a fear of failure. Wherever possible, performance management and development processes should re-enforce and reward people for what they can do rather than focusing on sanctions and critical feedback for when something goes wrong. Inherent in this is an understanding that, if someone is no longer delivering to their full potential, it's not necessarily their failure. It may be a failure of the environment to enable them.

> **Managers can be encouraged to consider and explore these questions.**
> - 'What does this person need from us to continue to thrive and perform?'
> - 'What are they doing right, when are things going well, and what has enabled that?'

> ▶ 'How can we celebrate the successes and learn from these?'

Sometimes, menopause will create a genuine mismatch between a woman's way of working and the demands faced in the role. Although a strengths-based approach helps to build confidence, this is not an excuse simply to stick with what you know or what has worked before. Every woman should be encouraged to focus on her capacity to keep adapting and growing.

A growth mindset is hugely valuable when faced with a new set of challenges. This allows women to see themselves not only as they are but also with a greater appreciation of how they could be with the right opportunity, effort and support. Through growth and development, women can find new strategies for managing symptoms, new techniques for overcoming problems and can develop newfound wisdom and strengths not needed before.

> **Helpful questions for women to explore include:**
> ▶ 'How have you successfully adapted in the past?'
> ▶ 'How are you continuing to grow and adapt?'
> ▶ 'What are you learning from this experience that is helpful?'
> ▶ 'What strategies can you use to manage your particular symptoms?'
> ▶ 'What tools or techniques help you to counter the impact of your symptoms, e.g. planning tools?'
> ▶ 'What further learning or development could help you respond to the new challenges you face?'

> **Case study: Cargyll**
>
> In the process of delivering leadership coaching to senior executive women, talent, leadership and coaching specialists, Gill Graham at Cargyll, has noted a range of themes linked to menopause. Just when women are reaching the most senior roles in client organizations, they often report particular challenges with their confidence, motivation, anxiety, well-being and energy levels. Often these feelings are new to those being coached and appear unrelated to the challenges of their role. Coaching women at this stage of their lives and careers requires an individualized approach that helps women regain personal purpose and control, where they feel empowered to seek personal and practical support.

Reinforce positive role models

Role models help women to visualize how they can adapt to menopause and find new strengths and confidence in the face of change. Seeing others who have navigated menopause and managed to keep participating, performing, progressing and thriving shows what is possible.

If the role model is known to have had challenges along the way, but found strategies to get them through, then all the better. This shows that a difficult situation can be turned around and that it is not just the lucky ones who manage to cope. It gives women hope when they see others sharing stories of their own anxiety, brain fog, sleeplessness, etc., but how they have still managed to keep working and succeeding, albeit in a different way.

While inspirational women can be found in the public eye, the best role models may be closer to home within your own organization. Coaching conversations can help women identify their own role-models and re-focus on the positives that could emerge as they work through the menopause transition.

> **Case study: Siobhan O'Sullivan**
>
> In her book *My Life on Pause*,[219] Siobhan O'Sullivan shares her experiences with early menopause at the age of 31 due to primary ovarian insufficiency. She showcases her own route towards medical diagnosis and management and also the psychological strategies that have helped. Losing the opportunity to have children came as a shock and raised questions about Siobhan's identity and role in life. Greater still was the fear that others would view her as 'broken'. Siobhan was able to reframe her thinking, finding positive identities and relationships that she could embrace going forward alongside finding medical and holistic approaches to managing symptoms. Siobhan's story encourages all going through menopause to find a positive way forward and to focus on what they can do to help themselves. Many organizations aim to showcase such stories as an inspiration to others.

Resolve beliefs, emotions and habits that get in the way

A large part of helping women regain their lost confidence comes through positive psychology and the benefits of focusing on a more helpful and optimistic view of the challenges and possibilities. In practice, negative thinking about women, ageing and menopause can be a deeply entrenched mindset or habit we have absorbed through our lives.

Although negative views of menopause and of the menopause transition can be deep-set, it is possible through psychological coaching to help women turn this around. It is not the sort of coaching that a manager or colleague, or even a typical life coach, will be able to deliver unless they have had specialist training. However, your organization could direct employees towards experts who offer psychological coaching for menopause. Psychological coaching is similar to CBT. It can be used to challenge unhelpful beliefs, emotions and habits that get in the way of a woman's ability to succeed and which interfere with her mental well-being.

However, this does not mean that menopause struggles are only in the woman's mind. There may, nevertheless, be real barriers in the working world that, even with a positive frame of mind, make it hard to cope. Psychological coaching can also help women identify practical strategies. This might mean planning how to advocate for her needs and secure reasonable adjustments.

For example, when experiencing brain fog a woman might fear that the impact will be obvious to colleagues and clients, catastrophic for her career, and represent a permanent and irreversible change. Such thoughts can serve to increase the stress she is feeling and result in a downward spiral. Unhelpful strategies may be used such as just trying to hide it. Alternatively, through coaching, she might reframe her thoughts and beliefs to see this symptom as representative of a time-limited stage. She might re-consider what colleagues can actually see changing in her performance. She might put any visible changes into perspective, against a backdrop of enduring and emerging strengths. While changing how she thinks and feels, she might also identify practical strategies and tools for improving her concentration and planning; or for negotiating temporary changes in her work. She might seek to minimize distractions on those few days when brain fog is a genuine problem.

Psychological coaching may include some of the following questions (although it takes some skill to guide a person through this process):

- 'What is happening for you that feels difficult?'
- 'In what way is menopause creating a challenge for you at work?'
- 'What impact does that have on you? On your feelings? On your actions? On how others perceive you? On your ability to participate, perform, progress or thrive at work?'
- 'Where the impact is negative for you, in what way could your thinking, mindset or actions contribute to this less helpful outcome?'
- 'What would be a more helpful outcome?'
- 'In what way could you influence your thinking, mindset, or the actions you take, to help you secure this more positive outcome?'
- 'Where are you already practising that?'
- 'Where might you need to secure support or a change from others?'
- 'What will you do now?'

Case study: JBA Consulting

This environmental and engineering consultancy has been looking to empower senior female staff through their later careers. Currently 38% of their 700 staff are women with 50 of these women aged 45 and over.

> The firm recognize that women's confidence can be impacted by a range of issues relating to gender, health, and ageing. In response they have initiated regular workshops to support this group, helping them find strategies for maximizing their potential and for sustaining their career progression. Brew People delivered a workshop uncovering how menopause can impact confidence at work, where attendees could also share their own personal challenges. They came away with a range of actions for sustaining confidence at work, building on the M-POWERED framework.

At the heart of empowerment is restoring women's belief that they can be effective, that they have the capability to meet the demands they face, and that they can learn how to deal with new challenges and barriers.

Key actions in Chapter 9

1. Help women to explore who they are now and what is important to them.
2. Help women to focus on their enduring and emerging strengths.
3. Help women to tap into their capacity for adaptation and growth.
4. Take care not to penalize women for difficulties arising from menopause.
5. Reflect on what individuals need from the organization to unleash their performance and potential.

6. Showcase inspirational role models to demonstrate what is possible through menopause.

7. Help women to adopt a positive mindset and to challenge unhelpful thinking and behaviours.

10
Relationships: supportive, trusting *relationships* and culture

It is impossible to overstate the importance of creating empowering relationships, where women know they can trust in others for support. These relationships might be enjoyed through networked communities within and beyond the organization. They might be individual connections with colleagues and allies. Of critical importance is the relationship between employee and their manager who acts as a conduit of support and practical help.

Strong relationships build a sense of safety and belonging that has a powerful protective effect for women facing menopause challenges. They counter the feelings of isolation that are common in menopause. However, they also offer opportunities where women can, share, listen, learn and problem-solve. When set within a broader menopause-friendly culture, women can trust that unhelpful behaviours will be challenged and not be allowed to undermine the positive impact of others.

In this chapter, I provide a guide for developing the knowledge, skills and opportunities that are needed to build empowering relationships and a menopause-friendly community. With a wide range of roles to play and a wide range of knowledge and attitudes to work with, I outline strategies for change.

Develop menopause awareness and skills

Empowering relationships are more likely where colleagues and managers share an understanding of menopause and its challenges. In Chapter 7, we heard that curiosity and a non-judgmental attitude is enough to get conversations started. Even so, people will feel more confident talking about menopause and taking action where they have some foundation knowledge and skills.

Later, we see there are a number of roles that people can play in building a menopause-friendly community. Each of these will have different demands:

- Some require greater insight into the strategic impact of menopause in the organization.
- Others may need to understand the practical dos and don'ts.
- Most will benefit from getting comfortable with the language around menopause and in being able to discuss it with confidence.
- Everyone will need some help in understanding what menopause is, why this is an issue in the workplace, and what they can do to help.
- For women themselves, the priority may be raising awareness of how menopause could impact them and what options they might have for accessing support with symptoms or addressing challenges at work.
- There is a growing wealth of learning resources to access on menopause. Many organizations will simply signpost these. Others know that running their own in-house training sends a clear message that this is important and makes it easier to ensure that everyone has got the message.

In delivering training, there's a place for:

- Expert voices, with up-to-date research and organizational trends.
- In-house practitioners who can spell out actions to be taken.
- Women who might share their menopause experiences with others.
- Senior leaders to show top level commitment to change.

Knowing your organization and the people you need to engage, what knowledge and skills will they need to play their part? How might you target different training opportunities and resources at different groups? What budget do you have to work with and what would deliver the biggest impact with that? Most critically, how will you ensure that greater awareness leads action?

> **What is your organization doing to develop the knowledge and skills that are fundamental to a culture shift?**
>
> ▶ How can you help people understand what menopause is and women's varied experiences of symptoms and their impact at work?
>
> ▶ What insight can you share that could help women access options for managing and reducing the symptoms they experience?
>
> ▶ How can you raise awareness of what is needed for a more menopause-friendly environment and options that help manage the impact of menopause?
>
> ▶ How can you help develop people's skills and confidence in talking about menopause?
>
> ▶ What would help people identify the specific role they can play?
>
> ▶ How can you sponsor and support those who want to take action in the light of what they are learning?

Case study: Unilever

Unilever position their menopause actions from a well-being perspective, ensuring that everyone has the right support in place to enable them to thrive at work. Achieving this means up-skilling managers and allies to have the right conversations, where further expert support can be signposted, and to identify what resources could help. Unilever was the first FMCG company to become menopause-friendly accredited, by demonstrating a wide range of actions and ongoing support. Success has been supported by their work in listening to employees, encouraging open conversations, and sharing information to raise awareness and enable personalized adjustments.[220,221]

Reinforce a menopause-friendly culture

As you shape a more menopause-friendly workplace, it becomes critical to build a culture that supports this aim. A range of actions can help to shift culture. Some of these may be top-down mandating others to be more supportive to those experiencing menopause. However, change is often more powerful when it is ignited within people, who themselves grow to see the value of change, understand the alternative mindsets that support change, and can see change as achievable.

One difficulty in igniting culture change is that people in the organization will not have the same starting points in terms of awareness or mindset and may have different individual responses to the prospect of change. A culture change programme will seek to work with this spectrum, nudging everyone in the same overall direction.[222]

The easiest change is with those who are ready and waiting to do more. They may already understand that being menopause friendly is important and want to play their part. They just don't yet know how. All they need is information and the skills to implement what they have learned. This might come from training and resources that you offer internally. But the most motivated may be eager to experiment, looking outside the organization to see what else can be done. Learning, and being allowed to try things out, are critical for change to get started. Your task is to harness their enthusiasm, securing sponsorship to support any actions this pioneering group seek to take.

Unfortunately, when it comes to culture change, people rarely push for something new or eagerly leap when the opportunity arises. Most people are inclined to sit on the fence and just think about it until they sense that a change has become a new norm. They may feel more comfortable sticking to what is familiar and 'how we do things round here'. This middle majority is more likely to let go of old ways of thinking and behaving if they see others adopting change and new norms developing. This is especially true where key influencers and decision-makers role model the new culture. A range of nudges that influence the middle majority to change in line with the new culture can include:

- Seeing new attitudes and behaviours become part of the group's identity. Most people don't like to feel left out.
- Seeing change as a natural extension of other practices. Most people feel more comfortable if change doesn't seem radical.
- Seeing key role models think and do things differently. If they are doing it, then they are likely to reward others who follow suit.
- Seeing the benefits to women, the organization and society as a whole if change is achieved.

What will your organization do to initiate and build momentum around menopause and develop a broader cohort of support?

- What information, research and online learning can be signposted for those who want or need to know more?

> ▸ What group training can be offered to raise shared knowledge and awareness, and prompt engagement among those not already interested?
>
> ▸ How will you highlight that change is already happening, or that this is simply an extension of other accepted changes?
>
> ▸ How will you communicate that being menopause friendly has become the accepted new norm?
>
> ▸ What will your leaders and key influencers be seen and heard doing to show this is a new expectation and practice?
>
> ▸ What role models or messaging will help to reinforce more positive associations with menopause and the capability and potential of older women?

However successful your organization is at enabling and encouraging change, there will always be those who remain resistant. They may hold concerns over the negative impact that changes could bring for the organization or, more specifically, for themselves. They may resist the notion that change could bring something better. They may be impervious to the power of the majority and prefer to set themselves apart as independent of normative influence. There will always be those who remain steadfastly loyal to old established ways of viewing the world and of old established practices.

For this group, the change strategy needs to incorporate different tactics again, providing rewards or a very clear signal of 'what's in it for me' that make change more personally worthwhile. Ultimately, and as a last resort, it may mean introducing penalties or censure for those who continue to counteract the essential change. The potential for organizations to be challenged and held accountable for their legal obligations on menopause, means that organizations are fully justified in mandating and enforcing new standards. Within your organization this may mean spelling out:

- Any language or demeaning treatment that would be regarded as unacceptable.
- The minimum standards that must be followed in various key decisions or processes, e.g. within recruitment, access to development opportunities, promotion or reward.

> **What will your organization do to counter resistance around menopause?**
>
> - How will you celebrate the benefits to everyone of working in a more menopause-friendly organization?
> - How can you communicate the 'What's in it for me?' of instituting changes?
> - What can you do to communicate the essential behaviours expected of all employees in relation to menopause and highlight what behaviours will be sanctioned?
> - What can your organization do to clarify the standards that must be met within key decisions and processes to evidence that these have been done in a menopause-friendly way?
> - What system does your organization have in place for raising complaints or responding to breaches of acceptable behaviour or practice?

Build and connect the community

It takes a village to deliver systemic change, covering between them a wide range of roles and actions. It helps if you can clarify what roles different people can plan and what is needed for this, ensuring as mentioned above that each group has access to the required knowledge and skills.

Women experiencing menopause

Women experiencing menopause cannot change how the organization operates without the involvement of the wider change community described earlier. However, they do, of course, play a key role in advocating for their own and others' needs. Simply by being connected to one another and part of an active group, women will feel emboldened to speak out more and get the help they need. For some it is enough to learn that they are not alone in their experiences and that fellow menopause warriors have their back. For others, they will learn most from those who have been there before and can share insight of how they navigated menopause within your organization.

To build and connect a community on menopause, you could:

- Build a *menopause network* connecting women.
- Consider retaining *women-only* events and channels to encourage greater openness.
- Offer *tools and events* for information sharing and dialogue.
- Offer opportunities for women to connect with male allies.
- Provide deeper *one-to-one empowerment focused coaching*.

Senior leadership

Senior leaders play a role in sponsoring the change. They ensure that the organization is leveraging older women to their full potential and put in place the budget, people and resources to make change possible. They hold the organization to account in delivering its policy commitments on menopause.

Get these people involved from the outset and keep them close as you progress.

Menopause champions

Champions can take the lead in the implementation and be particularly valuable playing the role of internal expert. They bring additional knowledge and research from outside the organization. They generate pace and focus among other leaders to sustain change. They play a key role in shaping communications both internally and externally to build social momentum. They keep listening and observing what works or doesn't work in achieving the menopause aims and feed this back to the business.

Often champions are volunteers who struggle to fit this role in on top of their usual day job. What can you do to support them with resources or by releasing them from day-to-day tasks?

People managers

People managers will play an essential front-line role in delivering change. They must reinforce positive behaviours within the team and exemplify these in their own actions. They will also be responsible for changing processes and practices to be more menopause friendly, delivering these in a consistent way.

It is managers who will have the greatest opportunity to talk with women experiencing menopause, challenge the taboo and offer emotional and practical support. Asking them to take this on could be seen as an extra burden in an already complex role. They will want to know that the extra responsibility is recognized, and balanced relative to other priorities.

Specialist coaches

Coaches can maximize the empowerment that comes via menopause conversations. They work with women to understand their situation and needs and to explore both psychological strategies and practical support. Such conversations require a level of skill beyond your typical manager. It can help to have specific managers, champions or HR practitioners trained as expert menopause coaches, or to lean into external menopause coaching providers.

Allies

Everyone in the organization can play their part as an ally. They can step up to challenge, encourage, or speak up on behalf of women experiencing menopause. They can show care and consideration for women facing menopause, with an aim to listen, understand and empower. Their voices help reframe this as a shared challenge rather than a challenge that older women must sort out for themselves.

The stronger and more diverse the foundation of support, the easier it is for leadership to shift the cultural norms. For this you may need to focus particular effort in attracting the support of men. It can help to run some men-only training and discussion groups on menopause to encourage participation.

External experts and groups

External experts can be a vital source of information, and support as your organization learns more about menopause and the actions it can take. This is a developing area. You do not have to re-invent the wheel, but it is unrealistic for everyone in your organization to become an expert. Find at least one person who is connected to the wider world of menopause at work and who can signpost resources and the latest best practice examples to the rest of your menopause change community. Alternatively, connect with an external expert provider that can act as a guide on your organization's menopause journey.

> **Your organization may need to put in place a variety of actions that reach these different groups and which give community members the knowledge skills and opportunities they need:**
>
> ▶ What information, research and online learning can be signposted for those who want to know or need to know more about the role they can play?
>
> ▶ How could employee resource groups help encourage dialogue, build allyship, and create an environment where women can secure emotional and practical support?
>
> ▶ How could one-to-one coaching develop individual confidence and empowerment among women experiencing menopause or for leaders trying to navigate their new role in delivering change?

Case study: Specsavers

With a 70% female workforce spread over joint-venture partner stores in 12 countries, Specsavers have had a strong focus on de-sensitizing conversations about menopause. A colleague network group (CNG) has

> helped to spread awareness and support, providing a safe space to listen, engage and to empower women experiencing menopause. However, it is recognized that women experiencing menopause may find it difficult to take the lead in championing action due to the impact of their own symptoms. Therefore, it has been critical to include a wide range of CNG members as ambassadors, champions and allies, with a clear understanding of their different roles in supporting change.[223,224]

People are stronger when they feel connected to and supported by others. Women who work through menopause will be more empowered when there is a menopause-friendly community and culture around them and a wide range of people playing their part.

Key actions in Chapter 10

1. Identify the different role people can play in a menopause-friendly community.

2. Develop knowledge and skills that enable a wide range of people to take action menopause.

3. Leverage the energy and commitment of those who are keen to do more.

4. Build momentum by showcasing successes and any changing expectations.

5. Counter resistance by illustrating the shared benefits of menopause actions.

6. Clarify behaviours and practices that are now mandatory.

7. Organize training, network groups, community events and one-to-one opportunities that enable everyone to learn, to open up conversations, and where women can secure support.

11
Environment: menopause-friendly physical *environment*

Many factors in the working environment can make life difficult when experiencing menopause. Your organization must shift towards designing workplaces with menopause in mind. The aim is to pre-empt problems and ensure women are comfortable, can manage their symptoms with dignity, and are protected from harm.

It can be a slow process to rethink and redesign work equipment and clothing, and safety measures. Furthermore, women may each want and need different adaptations. With that in mind it is vital that each woman is encouraged to voice her individual needs, and that practical solutions explored to meet these.

A range of adjustments can be made to where, when, and how people work (explored in Chapter 8). When specifically looking at the physical environment, there are multiple ways to make this menopause friendly. Four key actions stand out:

1. Helping women to keep cool and hydrated as a result of hot flushes.

2. Providing spaces for women to take time out during the day.

3. Ensuring adequate sanitary care for women experiencing difficult menstrual bleeding.

4. Reducing physical strain and other health and safety risks.

In this chapter, I provide a guide for adapting the physical environment. This includes ensuring facilities and equipment are designed with menopause in mind, that reasonable adjustments are offered in response to individual need, and that you carry out appropriate consultation and risk assessments to avoid potential harm.

Keep it cool

Hot flushes are one of the most well-recognized symptoms of menopause. They occur due to hormone changes impacting women's biological thermostat. A hot flush comes out of the blue and may only last a few minutes. However, the experience can be intense with a woman feeling extremely hot, with a flushed complexion, and sudden perspiration or sweating. Alongside this, women can experience a more rapid heartbeat and feelings of anxiety. Not every woman experiencing menopause will have hot flushes, but for some they can be debilitating. There can be cultural and ethnic differences, with more severe hot flushes for women of African-Caribbean ethnicity.[225]

Women can feel very embarrassed by the incidence of a hot flush as it is a visible sign of their menopausal state. It can be very uncomfortable, but worse, others often treat it as a cause for amusement. Women often feel that by exhibiting hot flushes, they may lose credibility in the workplace. The seen and unseen aspects of a hot flush are disruptive and can significantly undermine a woman's confidence.

To help women lessen the impact of hot flushes, adjustments should be offered that help to keep women cool and minimize embarrassment when one does occur. Flexing to the needs of individual women must be balanced with maintaining an environment that is sufficiently warm and comfortable for others. However, sticking a fan on a desk or changing the uniform for one older female member of staff could draw more unwelcome attention to that individual. Be driven by what your employees want. Options include:

- ▸ Flexing any uniform requirements ensuring that fabrics do not worsen feelings of overheating or make any sweating more obvious.

- Exploring options for improving ventilation either for all staff or providing additional fans or a window desk for those who need it.

- Providing easy and regular access to refreshments – including cool water as hot flushes can result in dehydration.

If a woman volunteers that she is finding work situations difficult as a result of hot flushes, then perhaps ask:

- 'What are the situations where this is most difficult for you?'

- 'What changes might help lessen the impact?'

- 'Is there anything that colleagues could do to make it feel less difficult?'

Case Study: West Mercia Police

Female police officers and staff can experience a range of challenges as a result of menopause symptoms. Depending on their specific roles, this can impact women's comfort, well-being and their confidence in carrying out duties. Night shifts, managing high stress situations, uncomfortable uniforms, and limited access to toilet and wash facilities can all be problematic. Supervisors are given access to a Menopause Risk Assessment tool to help staff identify any symptoms affecting them. This is followed by support in agreeing reasonable adjustments such as changes in shift patterns, additional breaks, improved ventilation or changes in uniform. West Mercia continue

> to work with other forces and external experts for example, with new uniform designs.

Keep it calm

Dealing with menopause symptoms at work can be stressful and exhausting. Women may be fighting to mask their condition, may have to exert extra effort to counteract brain fog or anxiety, or may simply be feeling stressed and exhausted directly because of hormonal changes. There are times when women experiencing menopause may feel an overwhelming need to sleep in the day. They may experience surges of emotion that are hard to manage. However, in an open-plan office or factory, or in a customer-facing role, it may be difficult to take just a few minutes to switch off and find balance again.

One reasonable adjustment that can make a significant difference for some women is allowing more regular breaks in the day. Ideally, this should allow the woman to get away to a quiet safe space. This will enable recovery time where a woman can recharge her batteries or allow her emotions to reset before getting back to her role.

Where women explain that they find it hard to keep going through an entire day or shift, perhaps ask them:

- ▶ 'Where and when are you able to take breaks during the day?'
- ▶ 'What would help you recharge your energy more effectively through the day?'
- ▶ 'How would you prefer to manage your time to enable additional rest breaks?'

Keep it discrete and convenient

Although menopause is reached when menstrual bleeding stops, there can be years of persistent, heavy or chaotic bleeding leading up to this point. This can present a range of challenges for women who must control and contain their bleeding and must also cope with any potential anaemia that follows. Sometimes bleeding is very sudden and very heavy, and no amount of protection is enough, creating risk of leaks through clothing.

Women have a right to be provided with adequate toilet, changing and wash facilities. However, they also have the right to be treated with dignity and respect when experiencing what can be an emotionally challenging situation. This last point is even more critical when considering the needs of trans men who may be using male toilets and may also be menstruating.

> **How will your organization ensure that difficulties with bleeding are treated with compassion and that facilities are adequate?**
>
> ▶ Can women easily access clean toilet facilities at regular points of the day or at short notice?
>
> ▶ Are sanitary wear dispensers and bins provided so that women can deal with unexpected bleeding and discretely dispose of waste?
>
> ▶ Can you offer free or subsidized period products to ensure all can access these whenever needed?
>
> ▶ Can you offer locker space near toilets and wash facilities so that women can change, if necessary, during the day without drawing attention to themselves?
>
> ▶ Can women discretely access a change of clothing or uniform when needed?

Problems with bleeding can be a difficult subject for a woman to raise at work due to embarrassment about menstruation, particularly within certain cultures. Therefore, it is important that these reasonable adjustments are made irrespective of whether an individual has requested it. Having said that, some consultation may help you design something appropriate for your employees.

> **These questions could be put to staff via a confidential survey, if not within staff conversations:**
>
> ▶ 'How satisfied are you with the toilets and sanitary care provided here?'
>
> ▶ 'Are you able to take toilet breaks whenever you need them?'
>
> ▶ 'What could make it easier for you when menstruating?'
>
> ▶ 'Are there any additional sanitary care needs you are experiencing at work as a result of the menopause transition?'

Keep it safe

As an employer you will have a duty to minimize any health and safety risk to employees from work. However, the focus on this will need to be even stronger for women experiencing menopause, with proactive strategies that protect women's health. Prevention is key in relation to your duties on health and safety. However, actions must also be taken when a woman raises this, themselves, as a risk area. Unfortunately, too often risks are not given sufficient attention and, as a result, women suffer a disproportionately high level of work-induced sickness.[226]

> **You will need to:**
>
> ▶ Carry out risk assessments that cover specific areas of risk.[227]
>
> ▶ Consult your employees or their representatives (as appropriate for the size of business) to gather insight on possible adjustments.
>
> ▶ Record any work-related health problems so these can be monitored, reported, and acted on.
>
> ▶ Keep detailed record of conversations, meetings and agreed options or next steps.

During the menopause transition, work can exacerbate a range of menopause symptoms, and therefore represent a health and safety issue such as these:

▶ **Musculo-skeletal disorders:** 71% of menopausal women experience musculoskeletal pain[228] with an increased risk from repetitive physical tasks, manual handling and lifting, or from spending too long in fixed positions or on their feet. Very often the roles women perform are those that can exacerbate musculoskeletal disorders: sitting at desks; working on keyboards; repetitive factory processes; standing in shops; or lifting (a significant issue for health workers and carers).

▶ **Hot flushes:** as discussed earlier, these can be made worse by poor ventilation or clothing. While being uncomfortable and debilitating, they also have the potential to lead to serious health issues because of dehydration.

▶ **Sleep disruption:** can be made worse by a lack of natural light and by unhelpful shift patterns. This can lead to brain fog and increase risks of accidents when using machinery or toxic chemicals at work.

Poor mental health is a common feature of menopause but is worsened where there is an unsupportive work culture leading to increased absences from work and potential risks within the workplace.

> **The following questions could help to identify options for reducing any health and safety risks through menopause:**
>
> ▶ 'What changes are you experiencing as a result of menopause that make it harder for you to carry out physical aspects of your role?'
>
> ▶ 'How does your work, or the processes or equipment you use impact your health and well-being?'
>
> ▶ 'What additional health and safety risks or accidents have you experienced in carrying out your role?'
>
> ▶ 'How could we adapt any processes or the equipment to reduce any strain or the risks you are exposed to?'
>
> ▶ 'What options could we explore for improving the health and safety impact of your work?'

> **Case study: Network Rail**
>
> Network Rail was recognized as a 'Times Top 50 Employer for Gender Equality' in 2024. The organization runs several initiatives including a Menopause Toolkit, which has been made publicly accessible.[229,230] The toolkit shares information and insight, with guidance on how to handle conversations about menopause. Line managers are encouraged, where needed, to carry out risk assessments and to help women experiencing menopause to explore reasonable adjustments such as flexible working, a more comfortable working space, additional changes of uniform, or menopause-friendly PPE. Safety critical clothing is offered in fabrics and styles specifically designed to enable women to keep cool and comfortable.

Sensitive design of spaces, clothing, equipment and work processes all play their part in enabling women to sustain performance and well-being through menopause and to keep safe. Where there is an individual need, women should be encouraged to speak up and reasonable adjustments explored.

> **Key actions in Chapter 11**
>
> 1. Consider environmental design changes to pre-empt difficulties through menopause.
> 2. Help women keep cool and hydrated.
> 3. Ensure women have the chance for time out to rest and recover.

4. Provide discrete and convenient access to toilets, wash facilities, and clothes changes.
5. Carry out health and safety risk assessments with menopause-related risk in mind.
6. Encourage women to speak up about any new risks or health impacts.
7. Explore individual reasonable adjustments and options for introducing these sensitively.

12
Delivery: sustainable and systemic *delivery*

The M-POWERED framework breaks down the key elements to include in your menopause action plan. To deliver these effectively they need to be pulled together into a cohesive whole. It might be tempting to choose actions using a simple pick-and-mix approach, hoping this will deliver change. It might feel easier just to replicate what another employer is doing. To deliver more meaningful change that connects to your organization's own strategy, you will benefit from a more rounded and integrated plan that directs and sustains progress.

Your plan needs a clear focus but cannot be too rigid as it must flex with our evolving understanding of menopause and the role that organizations can play. Actions must be tied together by a common thread ensuring they deliver an additive impact on menopause rather than counteracting one another. Finally, you will need to know how you are doing and be able to report your progress along the way.

In this chapter, I provide a guide for planning the delivery of a menopause action plan. This includes thinking through how to initiate the project and deliver sustainable action. It provides guidance for achieving systemic change by integrating menopause objectives through multiple policies and practices. Finally, it outlines ideas for monitoring progress.

Start with the beginning, middle and the end in mind

'Failing to plan is planning to fail', so they say. Every action plan calls for an agreed method for delivering the plan. This means defining: what, when, how and by whom it will be achieved:

- ▶ We have a desired end-goal: to be menopause friendly.
- ▶ We have measures of success: the equity of outcomes for women experiencing menopause; and the equity of experiences reported by women themselves.

- What is not so clear is how long it is going to take, and how multiple actions will be delivered alongside other organizational pressures.

If you lean towards a more structured approach to life, you may feel a strong urge to nail down the delivery plan: committing to an end goal and laying out the detailed steps that will get you there. There is certainly a place for that. Your sponsors will need to know what they are signing up for and what resources need to be ring-fenced to enable this to happen. Further with the wide range of actions to consider, it would be easy to become lost in the woods of delivery unless priority actions are specified, with clear accountabilities and timelines agreed. Chances are without a plan, progress will drift, with actions forever parked under those 'too difficult' or 'there's always tomorrow' banners.

The difficulty with complex culture change is that the route towards success is not easy to predict. We may not reach our menopause goals for years. However, in that time, our understanding of menopause and how to help keeps deepening. The context of political and economic pressures on organizations and women keeps shifting. The ability of women to access medical and psychological support outside of work continues to evolve. Furthermore, the people in your team keep changing and with that their readiness and ability to do what is needed.

Classic project management typically follows a 'waterfall' approach, that cascades tasks in a linear sequence. This contrasts to the increasingly common 'agile' approach, which is more flexible and iterative. Marrying the best of these methods you might:

- Build flexibility and pace into planning while staying true to an overall purpose and delivery structure.
- Start with quick wins, experiment and learn.
- Constantly engage stakeholders and secure feedback.

- ▶ Encourage short term pushes and celebrations of success along the way.
- ▶ Frequently re-orient in the light of a changing context.
- ▶ Maybe even revise the desired end in the light of any learning gained.

Finding the right balance of planning and experimentation will be specific to your organization. Large scale investment that impacts many staff may require more visioning and control. On the other hand, a smaller organization may dip its toe in the water with a relatively small-scale action and then plan next steps based on learning from this, allowing its approach to evolve more organically.

> **Thinking about your organization's menopause action plan and the need for both structure and agility:**
>
> - ▶ What is the strategic aim?
> - ▶ Who will deliver this and what are they accountable for?
> - ▶ What actions can be taken in the short, medium and longer term?
> - ▶ How will you ensure you stay on track?
> - ▶ How will the direction of travel and the actions for getting there be reviewed?
> - ▶ Where can you get started, achieving a quick win, or simply experimenting with something new?
> - ▶ Who do need to keep engaged and informed?

> **Case study: Dean Close Foundation**
>
> This family of independent schools and nurseries has a staff roll of 800, many of whom will be impacted by menopause personally, or in relation to colleagues. The school has initiated a menopause programme across its multiple sites. To begin with, this has centred around speaker events and regular menopause coffee sessions that provide a safe space for discussing menopause challenges, sharing possible solutions, and enjoying important community support. Attendees have developed greater confidence in raising their individual menopause needs with colleagues. This might be as simple as asking to take a few moments out to fetch a drink, taking cooler flasks of water into class, or agreeing additional ventilation.

Establish a menopause 'golden thread'

As we've said, becoming menopause friendly goes deeper than adding an awareness workshop or a stand-alone menopause policy. Women experiencing menopause will be found at all stages of the employee lifecycle and need to interact with your organization on many levels. At each of these touch points, your menopause-friendly approach will be put to the test.

Taking a systems-thinking approach, all changes to working practices should be integrated, so that positive actions taken in one area are not simply counteracted by outdated policies and structures elsewhere. This means establishing a clear menopause 'golden thread' that is woven through the fabric of how your organization operates.

Of course, it may not be practicable to up-end every aspect of your operations overnight. However, your organization will have a wide range of policies and programmes that will, in time, need to be consistent with your menopause aims. You will need to systematically review work structures, processes, and policies to ensure that these cater for women experiencing menopause.

> **As a start, your organization should review and refine the following:**
>
> ▶ EDI Policies: Do these cater for the unique challenges of menopause such as the role of intersectional risks and biases?
>
> ▶ H&S Policies: Do these cater for the specific health risks of menopause?
>
> ▶ Flexible Working Policy: Does this offer women the flexibility they want while balancing the impact on earnings and progression?
>
> ▶ Sickness and Absence Policy: Does this cater for the different patterns of intermittent, short term and long-term sickness absences?
>
> ▶ Disciplinary Policy/Performance Improvement Programme: Does this encourage exploration of reasonable adjustments before resorting to performance improvement or disciplinary measures?
>
> ▶ Wellness and Occupational Health Programmes: Does this cater for specialist menopause coaching or referrals to menopause health resources and experts?
>
> ▶ Employee Record Keeping Policy: Are you able to gather data on menopause while preserving confidentiality on private medical information?

Women experiencing menopause might interact with your organization at any stage of their career lifecycle. It is useful to revisit all these stages to create consistency.

> **For each of these career stages you will look to see:**
> ▶ Would women experiencing menopause receive equitable opportunities and treatment?
> ▶ Are they achieving equitable outcomes at each stage?
> ▶ In what ways could gendered ageism have a negative impact?
> ▶ What provision is there, to demonstrate that women will be supported through their menopausal experience?

> Take a look at the following employee lifecycle stages and how they might contribute to a fully integrated approach in your organization:
> ▶ **Talent attraction and retention:** Are you signalling menopause-friendly policies in job adverts and promoting a menopause-friendly brand? Are you living up to the promise so that women stay?
> ▶ **Selection:** Are you addressing gendered ageism in job criteria and helping hiring and promotion managers combat bias?
> ▶ **Onboarding:** Are you encouraging people to share their needs and exploring reasonable adjustments with them? Are you helping older women feel a sense of belonging?

- ▸ **Training and development:** Are you continuing to offer equitable access to development opportunities, or providing targeted coaching and development for women experiencing menopause?

- ▸ **Career progression:** Are you offering flexible working options and encouraging greater diversity at senior levels, for example by showcasing older female role models?

- ▸ **Performance management and reward:** Are you adjusting expectations on deliverables, targets and ways of working to be more inclusive? Are you maximizing women's impact and potential through menopause?

- ▸ **Redundancy and exit:** Are you taking extra care in how people are selected for redundancy, the conditions that might lead to dismissal, or tracking why women choose to leave?

Case study: Hays

As a customer and sales-focused organization, optimizing talent is key to the delivery of Hays' strategic mission. As part of this, the board share a clear commitment to DE&I and the well-being of its c.13,000 staff. Taking action on menopause is positioned within an inclusive approach to well-being. There is a strong intent to engage younger people and men, incorporating menopause issues within a wider programme of supporting hormonal health. Hays have launched drop-in sessions that provide a safe space for colleagues to share experiences and support.[231,232] Although guided by a strong social motive, Hays have continued to link the benefits back to the core commercial aims of the organization, helping to keep key stakeholders on board.

Keep an eye on progress

There's a lot to do to transform your organization and ensure it is menopause friendly. It will take time, but you can use a range of measures to understand progress. None of these will make sense unless you know exactly where you were when you started. It pays to carry out a full audit early on in your menopause journey and repeat this at regular intervals over subsequent years. Measuring how menopause friendly you are right now, provides a critical baseline against which you will later be able to evidence any future return on investment.

> Drawing on the key actions within Chapter 7, an audit will identify what outcomes have been achieved for women experiencing menopause by:
>
> ▶ Shining a light on menopause inequities.
>
> ▶ Evaluating women's perceptions and experiences.

For a full health check, your menopause audit should also include an assessment of what actions are currently being taken that would support a more menopause-friendly environment. Just as you would be asked by a doctor how much you drink or smoke or what your exercise and diet regime look like, so you should reflect on what actions and conditions are in place that might enable your organization to achieve its menopause goals. As far as possible you want your audit to point towards the things that could and should be changed rather than simply a measure of how things are.

> **Using the M-POWERED framework, what is already happening to support your organization's menopause action plan? Are those actions delivering what is needed? What else could be improved?**
>
> ▶ **Purpose:** Is everyone aligned and committed to a shared strategic purpose?
>
> ▶ **Openness:** Are people talking more about menopause and breaking down any taboo? Is data being gathered that reveals how things are and how it could be?
>
> ▶ **Will:** Are women being given the power to choose what works best for them? Are managers, coaches and colleagues using coaching style interactions to empower?
>
> ▶ **Effectiveness:** Are women being supported in giving their best through leveraging their strengths, building confidence and flexing their potential to adapt and grow?
>
> ▶ **Relationships:** Are people being given the skills and opportunities to play their part within a change community? Are women being provided with access to group and 1:1 support?
>
> ▶ **Environment:** Is the physical environment being made more comfortable and safer, with options for reasonable adjustments?

Carrying out a regular audit will give you a comprehensive picture of how things are going. This will enable you to report back to senior stakeholders and highlight the ROI achieved to date. There should also be opportunities to communicate actions and impacts along the way and through this help to maintain interest and momentum. Regular updates will also form the basis for refining plans on where you focus next.

When reporting progress on your action plan, consider:

- What positive changes or early wins can be reported and celebrated?

- What barriers are still to be addressed and how could you engage the help of stakeholders to resolve these?

- How can you ensure transparency and also maintain a positive mindset where progress might be difficult or slow?

For change to be achieved, delivery must be planned in a way that creates pace while staying focused on the overall purpose and aims. It can pay to experiment with individual actions. However, in the longer-term a wide range of policies and practices in your organization must work together in a systemic way. Progress should be tracked and celebrated, looking at the outcomes for women but also by evaluating the application of best practice principles captured in the M-POWERED framework.

Key Actions in Chapter 12

1. Experiment with easy wins that support your menopause aims.

2. Take an agile approach that enables you to learn, adapt and refocus as you progress.

3. Create structure with clear accountabilities to help keep progress on track.

4. Integrate your menopause aims through all related policies and practices.

5. Integrate your menopause aims through all stages of the employee life-cycle.

6. Measure progress via regular audits that look at: outcomes, experiences and current actions.

7. Share updates on progress to keep stakeholders engaged.

Conclusion

This book helps ensure your organization is set up to be menopause friendly, for today's and tomorrow's women. Even if this is a subject close to your heart and you have seen steps taken in the right direction, the chances are there is still more that could be done. Using the M-POWERED framework, you can make a real difference. It is based on organizational and psychological science and gets to the heart of what women need to participate, perform, progress and thrive during their menopause years.

While there is nothing new about menopause, in a work context menopause presents a radically different challenge not seen in any generation before. Employees may be generally getting older, but women have a unique set of health and lifestyle challenges as they reach this stage of life. At the same time, women represent the fastest-growing demographic in the workplace with many organizations depending on their talents to succeed. It simply makes good business sense to ensure that you can attract, retain and optimize this valuable source of talent.

It is hard to get a handle on what menopause is like and the impact that it has. No standard can be applied to all women, with experiences varying widely from the largely positive to the pathological. Hot flushes are not universal and are just one of a multitude of possible symptoms. Any action plan must cater for the wide range of individual needs and seek to be inclusive of different ages and ethnicities and, indeed, of different genders. What is clear, however, is that large numbers of people experiencing menopause feel unable to give their best at work: cutting down on their hours, holding back from promotions, paying the price with worsening physical or mental health; and simply quitting altogether.

There is pressure for organizations to do something about this. Pressure from women who want and need to keep working. Pressure from governments that need to maximize the economic activity of women and protect the health and well-being of society as a whole. Organizations are eager to move with the times and find a new equation for women who work.

There are many reasons why being menopause friendly is not a given. There has been a silence around the subject which leaves us ignorant of the challenges, and complacent about the consequences for women. There has been significant taboo and gendered ageism which stop us having those important conversations that could help. There are systemic flaws in our organizational systems which were simply not designed to create the best environment for women experiencing menopause.

As women are hit from all sides by hormonal changes, life challenges, and a working world that is too ready to write them off, they can falter. Women's motivation and engagement with work becomes fundamentally challenged by an erosion of empowerment. They can experience a loss of will or agency, see their old strengths or effectiveness compromised, and feel an increasing sense of 'otherness', struggling on without the benefit of supportive relationships. The challenges of change, and the negative associations of menopause can make it hard for women to maintain a positive mindset and to make the personal adaptations that could help.

However, the problem cannot be fixed by women doing all the work themselves. There are real barriers that even the most positive person would struggle to overcome. Organizations must equally play their part in ensuring that women can enjoy equitable opportunities and outcomes. They must take a strategic approach, delivering an action plan that is sustainable and which both directly addresses psychological empowerment in women, and which concurrently creates the right environment and relationships to enable empowerment.

There is complex culture and organizational change involved. Your organization will need some serious stakeholder support to deliver systemic change: shining a light on the need for change, ensuring women feel safe to ask for help, ensuring that when women do speak they are heard, building flexibility into organizational practices so that women can re-shape how they work; building a knowledgeable, skilled and supportive community; and yes, possibly even buying a few desk fans if that's what your women want.

Notes

[1] Garlick, D. (2018). *Menopause: the change for the better*. Bloomsbury Publishing.

[2] Madders, J., MP, Reynolds, J., MP, Rayner, A., MP, & Department for Business and Trade. (2024, 10 October). Government unveils significant reforms to employment rights [press release]. From: www.gov.uk/government/news/government-unveils-most-significant-reforms-to-employment-rights

[3] Throsby, K. & Roberts, C. (2024). Bodies of change: menopause as biopsychosocial process. In Beck, V. & Brewis, J . (eds), *Menopause transitions and the workplace*. Bristol University Press.

[4] Boys, J. & CIPD (2022). *Understanding older workers: analysis and recommendations to support longer and more fulfilling working lives* (report). Chartered Institute of Personnel and Development.

5 ageing-better.org.uk (n.d.). State of ageing in 2023. In State of *ageing*.

[6] Boys, J. & CIPD (2022). *Understanding older workers: analysis and recommendations to support longer and more fulfilling working lives* (report). Chartered Institute of Personnel and Development.

[7] Department for Work and Pensions (2023). Economic labour market status of individuals aged 50 and over, trends over time: September 2023.

[8] Edge, C. & Swift, E. (2024, 22 March). Ageing women's workplace wellbeing: a global political imperative.

[9] State pension age timetables (n.d.). In *GOV.UK*. https://assets.publishing.service.gov.uk/media/5a7f02e640f0b62305b84929/spa-timetable.pdf

[10] Francis-Devine, B., Hutton, G. & Commons Library (2024). Women and the UK economy. *Commons Library Research Briefing*, 6838.

[11] Fluchtmann, J., Keese, M. & Adema, W. (2024). Gender equality and economic growth. In *OECD Social Employment and Migration Working Papers*.

[12] Esteban Ortiz-Ospina, Sandra Tzvetkova and Max Roser (2018). 'Women's Employment'. Published online at OurWorldInData.org

[13] Seibel, M. & Seibel, S. (2022). *Working through menopause: The impact on women, businesses and the bottom line.* Bookbaby.

[14] Cleghorn, E. (2022). *Unwell women: misdiagnosis and myth in a man-made world.* Penguin.

[15] Goldin, C. (1988). Marriage bars: discrimination against married women workers, 1920s to 1950s. NBER Working Paper No. w2747.

[16] Palermo, G., D'Angelo. S, Ntani, G., Bevilacqua, G., Walker-Bone, K. (2024, 11 June) Work and retirement among women: the health and employment after fifty study. *Occup Med* (Lond). 74(4):313–322.

[17] Goldin, C., Kerr, S. P., Olivetti, C. & National Bureau of Economic Research (2022). *When the kids grow up: women's employment and earnings across the family cycle* (no. 30323).

[18] Roantree, B. & Vira, K. (2018). *The rise and rise of women's employment in the UK.* See https://ifs.org.uk/publications/rise-and-rise-womens-employment-uk

[19] Francis-Devine, B. (2023). *Average earnings by age and region.* From: https://commonslibrary.parliament.uk/. UK Parliament.

[20] White, N. J. & Office for National Statistics (2023). Gender pay gap in the UK: 2023. Statistical Bulletin.

[21] Ciminelli, G., Schwellnus, C. & Stadler, B. (2021). Sticky floors or glass ceilings? The role of human capital, working time flexibility and discrimination in the gender wage gap. *OECD Economics Department Working Papers*.

[22] Conti, G., Ginja, R., Persson, P. & Willage, B. (2024). *The menopause 'penalty.'* From: https://ifs.org.uk/publications/menopause-penalty

[23] Centre for Ageing Better. (2022). The State of Ageing 2022. From: https://ageing-better.org.uk/sites/default/files/2022-04/The-State-of-Ageing-2022-online.pdf

[24] Benny, L., Institute for Social and Economic Research, Bhalotra, S., Department of Economics, University of Warwick, Fernández, M. & Facultad

de Economía, Universidad de los Andes. (2021). *Occupation flexibility and the graduate gender wage gap in the UK*.

[25] Cukrowska-Torzewska, E. & Matysiak, A. (2020). The motherhood wage penalty: a meta-analysis. *Social Science Research*, 88–89, 102416.

[26] Leopold, T. (2018). Gender differences in the consequences of divorce: a study of multiple outcomes. *Demography*, 55(3):769–797.

[27] Conti, G., Ginja, R., Persson, P. & Willage, B. (2024). *The menopause 'penalty.'* IFS.

[28] Zaidi, K. & Mirza-Davies, J. (2024). The gender pensions gap. In *Commons Library Research Briefing* (no. 9517).

[29] Office for National Statistics (ONS), released 9 November 2023, ONS website, statistical bulletin, Time use in the UK: September 2023.

[30] Fry, R., Aragao, C., Hurst, K. & Parker, K. (2023). In a growing share of U.S. marriages, husbands and wives earn about the same. In *Pew Research Center*.

[31] Ervin, J., Taouk, Y., Alfonzo, L. F., Hewitt, B. & King, T. (2022). Gender differences in the association between unpaid labour and mental health in employed adults: a systematic review. *The Lancet Public Health*, 7(9):e775–e786.

[32] Office for National Statistics (ONS), released 19 January 2023, ONS website, statistical bulletin, Birth characteristics in England and Wales: 2021.

[33] Age UK (2019). Breaking point. From: www.ageuk.org.uk

[34] Ryan, L. (2023). *Revolting women: why midlife women are walking out, and what to do about it*. Practical Inspiration Publishing, p. 62.

[35] NimbleFins (2024, 18 April). *Divorce Statistics UK* 2023.

[36] Family and its protective effect (2022). In R. De Souza, Part 1 of the Independent Family Review.

[37] Tupy, M. L. & Bailey, R. (2023, 1 March). *The changing nature of work*. Human Progress.

[38] Britannica, T. Editors of Encyclopaedia (2024, 18 July). Industrial Revolution. Encyclopedia Britannica. From: www.britannica.com/event/Industrial-Revolution

[39] Kellaway, L. (2022, 22 July). How the office was invented. BBC News. www.bbc.co.uk/news/magazine-23372401

⁴⁰ Wikipedia contributors. (2024, 18 July). History of labour law in the United Kingdom. In *Wikipedia, The Free Encyclopedia*. Retrieved 5 August 2024.

⁴¹ Imperial War Museums (n.d.). *12 things you didn't know about women in the first world war*. See point 11 on: www.iwm.org.uk/history/12-things-you-didnt-know-about-women-in-the-first-world-war

⁴² Autonomy team: Lewis, K., Stronge, W., Kellam, J., Kikuchi, L. Quantitative research team: Schor, Prof. J., Fan, Prof. W., Kelly, Prof. O., Gu, G. Qualitative research team: Frayne, Dr. D., Burchell, Prof. B., Bridson Hubbard, N., White, J., Kamarāde, Dr. D. & Mullens, F. (2023). *The results are in: the UK's four-day week pilot*. Autonomy Research Ltd.

⁴³ Matthews, T. A., Chen, L., Omidakhsh, N., Zhang, D., Han, X., Chen, Z., Shi, L., Li, Y., Wen, M., Li, H., Su, D. & Li, J. (2022). Gender difference in working from home and psychological distress – a national survey of U.S. employees during the COVID-19 pandemic. *Industrial Health*, 60(4):334–344.

⁴⁴ Chung, H. (2022). *The flexibility paradox: why flexible working leads to (self-) exploitation*. Policy Press.

⁴⁵ Sevilla, A. & Smith, S. (2020). Baby steps: the gender division of childcare during the COVID-19 pandemic. *Oxford Review of Economic Policy*, 36(Supplement_1):S169–S186.

⁴⁶ Williamson, S., Jogulu, U., Lundy, J. & Taylor, H. (2024). Will return-to-office mandates prevent proximity bias for employees working from home? *Australian Journal of Public Administration*.

⁴⁷ Peetz, D., Preston, A., Walsworth, S. & Weststar, J. (2023). COVID-19 and the gender gap in research productivity: understanding the effect of having primary responsibility for the care of children. *Studies in Higher Education*, 48(9):1428–1439.

⁴⁸ International Monetary Fund, Kochhar, K., Fabrizio, S., Kolovich, L., Newiak, M., Agarwal, A. & Yin, R. J. (2018). Pursuing women's economic empowerment (report). In *International Monetary Fund*.

⁴⁹ Sharma, K., Akre, S., Chakole, S. & Wanjari, M. B. (2022). Stress-Induced diabetes: a review. *Cureus*, 14(9):e29142.

⁵⁰ Cleghorn, E. (2022). *Unwell women: misdiagnosis and myth in a man-made world*. Penguin.

⁵¹ Rocha, A. L., Oliveira, F. R., Azevedo, R. C., Silva, V. A., Peres, T. M., Candido, A. L., Gomes, K. B. & Reis, F. M. (2019). Recent advances in

the understanding and management of polycystic ovary syndrome. F1000Research, 8, F1000 Faculty Rev-565.

[52] Gunter, J. (2024). *Blood: the science, medicine and mythology of menstruation.* Hachette UK.

[53] Dorofeev, D. (2022, 14 February). The role of estrogen in men's health. From: www.news-medical.net/

[54] Cooke, P. S., Jr., Nanjappa, M. K., Ko, C., Prins, G. S., Hess, R. A. (2017). Estrogens in male physiology. *Physiological Reviews*, 97:995–1043.

[55] Hammes, S. R. & Levin, E. R. (2019). Impact of estrogens in males and androgens in females. *J Clin Invest.*, 129(5):1818–1826.

[56] Hammes, S. R. & Levin, E. R. (2019). Impact of estrogens in males and androgens in females. *J Clin Invest.*, 129(5):1818–1826.

[57] Seibel, M. & Seibel, S. (2022). *Working through menopause: the impact on women, businesses and the bottom line.* Bookbaby.

[58] Schoenaker, D. A., Jackson, C. A., Rowlands, J. V. & Mishra, G. D. (2014). Socioeconomic position, lifestyle factors and age at natural menopause: a systematic review and meta-analyses of studies across six continents. *International Journal of Epidemiology*, 43(5):1542–1562.

[59] British Menopause Society (2023). *Menopause in ethnic minority women.*

[60] Mosconi, L. (2024). *The menopause brain: the new science empowering women to navigate midlife with knowledge and confidence.* Atlantic Books.

[61] Gartoulla, P., Worsley, R., Bell, R. J. & Davis, S. R. (2018). Moderate to severe vasomotor and sexual symptoms remain problematic for women aged 60 to 65 years. *Menopause*, 22(7):694–701.

[62] Bernhardt, L. & Lawson, C. A. (2019). Early menopause and risk of cardiovascular disease: an issue for young women. *The Lancet Public Health*, 4(11):e539–e540. From: https://doi.org/10.1016/s2468-2667(19)30184-7

[63] Mosconi, L. (2024). *The menopause brain: the new science empowering women to navigate midlife with knowledge and confidence.* Atlantic Books.

[64] Mimi Arquilla, E. (2023, 24 August). *Ask the expert: what to know about menopause when you're trans or nonbinary.* Healthline.

[65] Toze, M. & Westwood, S. (2024). Experiences of menopause among non-binary and trans people. *International Journal of Transgender Health*, 1–12.

[66] Antonio, L., Wu, F. C. W., Moors, H., Matheï, C., Huhtaniemi, I. T., Rastrelli, G., Dejaeger, M., O'Neill, T. W., Pye, S. R., Forti, G., Maggi, M., Casanueva, F. F., Slowikowska-Hilczer, J., Punab, M., Tournoy, J., Vanderschueren, D., Forti, G., Petrone, L., Corona, G., ... Korrovitz, P. (2022). Erectile dysfunction predicts mortality in middle-aged and older men independent of their sex steroid status. *Age and Ageing*, 51(4).

[67] Manchester University (2010, 17 June). *Researchers unzip symptoms of the 'male menopause'.* From: www.manchester.ac.uk/about/news

[68] McGregor, A. & The Migraine Trust (2022, 8 March). *Migraine and perimenopause.*

[69] Nombora, O., Rodrigues, T., Felgueiras, P., Silva, B. F. & Venâncio, Â. (2024). Menopause-associated Psychosis: a case report and literature review. *Psychiatry Research Case Reports*, 3(1):100210.

[70] Oppenheim, M. (2021, 6 October). Fear of being labelled hysterical: 1 in 10 women experience suicidal thoughts due to perimenopause. *Independent.*

[71] Newson Health (2021, 30 June). *Delayed diagnosis and treatment of menopause is wasting NHS appointments and resources.*

[72] Newson Health (2021, 30 June). Delayed diagnosis and treatment of menopause is wasting NHS appointments and resources.

[73] Mosconi, L. (2024). *The menopause brain: the new science empowering women to navigate midlife with knowledge and confidence.* Atlantic Books.

[74] Newson Health (n.d.). *Perimenopause and menopause symptoms explained.* From: www.newsonhealth.co.uk/menopause-symptoms/

[75] CIPD (2023). Menopause in the workplace: employee experiences in 2023. In CIPD (report). Chartered Institute of Personnel and Development.

[76] CIPD. (2023). Menopause in the workplace: employee experiences in 2023. In CIPD (report). Chartered Institute of Personnel and Development.

[77] Behrman, S. & Crockett, C. (2023). Severe mental illness and the perimenopause. *BJPsych Bulletin*, 1–7.

[78] Nakanishi, M., Endo, K., Yamasaki, S., Stanyon, D., Sullivan, S., Yamaguchi, S., Ando, S., Hiraiwa-Hasegawa, M., Kasai, K., Nishida, A. & Miyashita, M. (2023). Association between menopause and suicidal ideation in mothers of adolescents: a longitudinal study using data from a population-based cohort. *Journal of Affective Disorders*, 340:529–534.

[79] Newson, L., Newson Health Research and Education & The Menopause Charity. (n.d.). *Menopause and the workplace.*

[80] Woyka, J. & British Menopause Society (2024). *Non-hormonal-based treatments for menopausal symptoms.*

[81] Mosconi, L. (2024). *The menopause brain: the new science empowering women to navigate midlife with knowledge and confidence.* Atlantic Books.

[82] Newson Health Menopause Society (2022, 26 October). *Healthcare staff struggling with menopause symptoms are considering quitting, Newson Health survey finds.*

[83] Jehan, S., Jean-Louis, G., Zizi, F., Auguste, E., Pandi-Perumal, S. R., Gupta, R., Attarian, H., McFarlane, S. I., Hardeland, R. & Brzezinski, A. (2017). Sleep, melatonin, and the menopausal transition: what are the links? *Sleep Science*, 10(01):11–18.

[84] Conde, D. M., Verdade, R. C., Valadares, A. L. R., Mella, L. F. B., Pedro, A. O. & Costa-Paiva, L. (2021). Menopause and cognitive impairment: a narrative review of current knowledge. *World Journal of Psychiatry*, 11(8):412–428.

[85] Ayers, B. N., Forshaw, M. J. & Hunter, M. S. (2011, 23 May). The menopause. *The Psychologist.*

[86] British Menopause Society (2023). *Menopause in ethnic minority women.*

[87] Haridasani Gupta, A. (2023, 4 September). How menopause affects women of color. *New York Times.*

[88] Nagata, C. (2001). Soy product intake and hot flashes in Japanese women: results from a community-based prospective study. *American Journal of Epidemiology*, 153(8):790–793. From: https://doi.org/10.1093/aje/153.8.790

[89] Logan, S., Wong, B. W. X., Tan, J. H. I., Kramer, M. S. & Yong, E. L. (2023). Menopausal symptoms in midlife Singaporean women: prevalence rates and associated factors from the Integrated Women's Health Programme (IWHP). *Maturitas*, 178, 107853.

[90] Fang, Y., Liu, F., Zhang, X., Chen, L., Liu, Y., Yang, L., Zheng, X., Liu, J., Li, K. & Li, Z. (2024). Mapping global prevalence of menopausal symptoms among middle-aged women: a systematic review and meta-analysis. *BMC public health*, 24(1):1767.

[91] Bromberger, J. T. & Kravitz, H. M. (2011). Mood and menopause: findings from the study of Women's Health Across the Nation (SWAN) over 10 years. *Obstetrics and Gynecology Clinics of North America*, 38(3):609–625.

[92] Conde, D. M., Verdade, R. C., Valadares, A. L. R., Mella, L. F. B., Pedro, A. O. & Costa-Paiva, L. (2021). Menopause and cognitive impairment: a narrative review of current knowledge. *World Journal of Psychiatry*, 11(8):412–428.

[93] Menopause Support & British Menopause Society. (n.d.). *Understanding menopause: your essential guide to navigating menopause successfully*.

[94] Newman, T. (2024, 11 September). *Menopause: introducing a new way to understand your experience*. Zoe. From: https://zoe.com/learn/menoscale-calculator-menopause-research

[95] Garlick, D. (2018). *Menopause: the change for the better*. Bloomsbury Publishing.

[96] Newman, T. (2024, 11 September). *Menopause: introducing a new way to understand your experience*. Zoe.

[97] Ayers, B., Forshaw, M. & Hunter, M. S. (2010). The impact of attitudes towards the menopause on women's symptom experience: a systematic review. *Maturitas*, 65(1): 28–36.

[98] Menopause Support & British Menopause Society. (n.d.). *Understanding menopause: your essential guide to navigating menopause successfully*.

[99] Glynne, S., Kamal, A., Kamel, A. M., Reisel, D. & Newson, L. (2024). Effect of transdermal testosterone therapy on mood and cognitive symptoms in peri- and postmenopausal women: a pilot study. *Archives of Women S Mental Health*. From: https://doi.org/10.1007/s00737-024-01513-6

[100] Scott, A. & Newson, L. (2020). Should we be prescribing testosterone to perimenopausal and menopausal women? A guide to prescribing testosterone for women in primary care. *British Journal of General Practice*, 70(693):203–204. From: https://doi.org/10.3399/bjgp20x709265

[101] Hickey, M., LaCroix, A. Z., Doust, J., Mishra, G. D., Sivakami, M., Garlick, D. & Hunter, M. S. (2024). An empowerment model for managing menopause. The Lancet, 403(10430):947–957. From: https://doi.org/10.1016/s0140-6736(23)02799-x

[102] British Menopause Society & Robinson, L. (2023). HRT: the history. In *Women's Health Concern*, British Menopause Society. From: www.womens-health-concern.org/wp-content/uploads/2022/11/10-WHC-FACTSHEET-HRT-The-history-NOV22-A.pdf

[103] Ritchie, H. (2024, 2 July). Doctors dismissed these women as hysterical. Now they're fighting back. *BBC News*.

[104] Menopause Support. (2021, 13 May). *Menopause Support survey reveals shocking disparity in menopause training in medical schools.*

[105] Whiteley, J., DiBonaventura, M. D., Wagner, J., Alvir, J. & Shah, S. (2013). The impact of menopausal symptoms on quality of life, productivity, and economic outcomes. *Journal of Women S Health*, 22(11):983–990.

[106] CIPD (2023). Menopause in the workplace: employee experiences in 2023. In *CIPD* (report). Chartered Institute of Personnel and Development.

[107] Bazeley, A., Marren, C., Shepherd, A. & Fawcett Society. (2022). *Menopause and the workplace*. The Fawcett Society.

[108] Power, C. & Elliott, J. (2005). Cohort profile: 1958 British birth cohort (National Child Development Study). *International Journal of Epidemiology*, 35(1):34–41.

[109] Evandrou, M., Falkingham, J., Qin, M. & Vlachantoni, A. (2021). Menopausal transition and change in employment: evidence from the National Child Development Study. *Maturitas*, 143:96–104.

[110] Bryson, A., Conti, G., Hardy, R., Peycheva, D. & Sullivan, A. (2021). The consequences of early menopause and menopause symptoms for labour market participation. *Social Science & Medicine*, 293, 114676.

[111] Garlick, D. (2023, 4 July). *The business case for being menopause friendly*. HR Director.

[112] Price, A. (2024, 18 September). Labour's Menopause Action Plan: Why small companies should keep up or get left behind. *HR Zone*.

[113] Verdict. (2022, 10 March). *Social responsibility: Empowering menopausal women in the workplace.*

[114] Brewis, J., Beck, V., Davies, A. & Matheson, J. (2017). *The effects of menopause transition on women's economic participation in the UK*. Department for Education.

[115] Francis-Devine, B., Hutton, G. & Commons Library (2024). Women and the UK economy. *Commons Library Research Briefing*, 6838.

[116] Department for Work and Pensions (2023, September). Economic labour market status of individuals aged 50 and over, trends over time.

[117] Care Quality Commission (2023). *The state of health care and adult social care in England 2022/23.*

[118] The Strategy Unit and Health Economics Unit (2022). Menopause and the NHS workforce. In *The Strategy Unit*.

[119] Women in Technology and IT (n.d.). *6 Reasons Why So Many Women Leave Tech Jobs.*

[120] Oxford Economics and Unum (2014). *The cost of brain drain: understanding the financial impact of staff turnover.*

[121] Brewis, J., Beck, V., Davies, A. & Matheson, J. (2017). *The effects of menopause transition on women's economic participation in the UK.* Department for Education.

[122] Newson, L. & Lewis, R. (2021). Impact of perimenopause and menopause on work (paper presentation). Royal College of GP Annual Conference, London, UK.

[123] Credit Suisse Group AG (2012, 31 July). *Large-cap companies with at least one woman on the board have outperformed their peer group with no women on the-board by 26% over the last six years, according to a report by Credit Suisse Research Institute* (Press release).

[124] www.jaguarlandrover.com/diversity-equity-inclusion

[125] Nicholls, J., Lawlor, E., Neitzert, E., Goodspeed, T. & SROI Network (2012). *Guide to social return on investment.*

[126] Rochlin, S., Bliss, R., Jordan, S., Kiser, C. Y. & Project ROI Sponsors (2015). Defining the competitive and financial advantages of corporate responsibility and sustainability. In IO Sustainability & Babson College, *Project ROI: Defining the competitive and financial advantages of corporate responsibility and sustainability.*

[127] YouGov (2024). *Will Brits purchase from a brand based on the conditions of their worker?* From: https://yougov.co.uk/

[128] BUPA (2022). Gen Z seek ethical workplaces as environ-mental health burden bites.

[129] Cropanzano, R., University of Colorado Boulder, Bowen, D. E., University of Colorado Boulder, Gilliland, S. W. & The University of Arizona (2007). The management of organizational justice. In *Academy of Management Perspectives.*

[130] Bosch, A. (2024). Organizational and social justice paradoxes in EDI. *Frontiers in Psychology,* 15.

[131] Bashir, R. & Acuity Law (2023). *The true costs of employment tribunal claims.*

[132] Spencer Shaw (solicitors) (2023). When an employment law failing becomes a PR nightmare.

[133] www.gov.uk/employment-tribunal-decisions

[134] Wood, T. (2022). *A practical guide to the law in relation to menopause and perimenopause in the workplace.*

[135] Ms M. Rooney vs Leicester City Council EA-000070-DA.

[136] Cahn, N., Crawford, B. & Waldman, E. (2023). Millions of women are working during menopause, but US law isn't clear on employees' rights or employers' obligations. *The Conversation.*

[137] Lewis Silkin (2024, 6 February). *Labour plans changes to discrimination law.*

[138] Lewis Silkin (2024, 6 February). *Labour plans changes to discrimination law.*

[139] EHRC (2019, 25 November). *Direct and indirect discrimination.*

[140] EHRC (2018, 4 June). *Harassment and victimisation.*

[141] ACAS (2022, 25 March). *Menopause and the law.*

[142] Mrs M. Lynskey vs Direct Line Insurance Services Ltd: 1802204/2022 and 1802386/2022.

[143] Ms L. Best vs Embark on Raw Ltd: 3202006/2020.

[144] A. vs Bonmarche Ltd (in administration): 4107766/2019.

[145] Mrs K. Anderson (or Farquharson) vs Thistle Marine (Peterhead) Ltd and J. D. Clark: 4101775/2023.

[146] Ms M. Davies vs Scottish Courts and Tribunals Service: 4104575/2017.

[147] ACAS (2024). Code of Practice on requests for flexible working.

[148] Mrs A. Shearer vs South Lanarkshire Council: 4107433/2023.

[149] Seibel, M. & Seibel, S. (2022). *Working through menopause: the impact on women, businesses and the bottom line.* Bookbaby.

[150] Cleghorn, E. (2022). *Unwell women: misdiagnosis and myth in a man-made world.* Penguin.

[151] Commission on Older Women (2013). *The Commission on Older Women. Interim report.*

[152] Bruce, I. (2024, 8 March). *Brands fail to invest in women: analysing representation in advertising.* Creativex.

[153] Keeble-Ramsay, D. & Ridealgh, K. (n.d.). Silently dancing on the ceiling: women's workplace experiences peri-, menopausal and post-menopause in

the UK. In *CIPD*. CIPD Applied Research Conference 2017: The Shifting Landscape of Work and Working Lives.

[154] Clarke, L. H. & Korotchenko, A. (2011). Aging and the body: a review. *Canadian Journal on Aging = La revue canadienne du vieillissement*, 30(3):495–510.

[155] Burn, I. (2023, 2 March). *Job age discrimination for women starts at least 10 years earlier than for men*. University of Liverpool.

[156] Neumark, D., Burn, I., Button, P. & National Bureau of Economic Research (2015). Is it harder for older workers to find jobs? New and improved evidence from a field experiment (Working Paper 21669). National Bureau of Economic Research.

[157] Drydakis, Nick; Paraskevopoulou, Anna; Bozani, Vasiliki (2022). A field study of age discrimination in the workplace: the importance of gender and race. Pay the gap, GLO Discussion Paper, no. 1170, Global Labor Organization (GLO), Essen.

[158] Tahmaseb-McConatha, J., Kumar, V. K., Magnarelli, J. & Hanna, G. (2023). The gendered face of ageism in the workplace. *Advances in Social Sciences Research Journal*, 10(1).

[159] Mosconi, L. (2024). *The menopause brain: the new science empowering women to navigate midlife with knowledge and confidence*. Atlantic Books.

[160] Greer, G. (2018). *The change: women, ageing and the menopause*. Bloomsbury Publishing.

[161] Gunter, J. (2024). *Blood: the science, medicine and mythology of menstruation*. Hachette UK.

[162] Hasson, G. & Butler, D. (2020). *Mental health and wellbeing in the workplace: a practical guide for employers and employees*. John Wiley & Sons.

[163] Kale, S. (2021, 17 August). 'My bosses were happy to destroy me' – the women forced out of work by menopause. *The Guardian*.

[164] Cleghorn, E. (2022). *Unwell women: misdiagnosis and myth in a man-made world*. Penguin.

[165] Paludo, A. C., Paravlic, A., Dvořáková, K. & Gimunová, M. (2022). The effect of menstrual cycle on perceptual responses in athletes: a systematic review with meta-analysis. *Frontiers in Psychology*, 13.

[166] Odom, S., et al. (2021). Meta-analysis of gender performance gaps in undergraduate natural science courses. *CBE–Life Sciences Education*, 20(3):ar40.

[167] Brewis, J., Atkinson, C., Beck, V., Davies, A. & Duberley, J. (2020). Menopause and the workplace: new directions in HRM research and HR practice. *Human Resource Management Journal*.

[168] Perez, C. C. (2020). *Invisible women: exposing data bias in a world designed for men*. Chatto & Windus.

[169] Steffan, B. & Loretto, W. (2024). *Menopause, work and mid-life: challenging the ideal worker stereotype*. Gender Work and Organization.

[170] British Occupational Hygiene Society: the Chartered Society for Worker Health Protection. (2023). *Uncovering the UK's hidden crisis in women's workplace health* (p. 1).

[171] Westover, J. (2021, 10 December). *The role of systems thinking in organizational change and development*. Forbes.

[172] Lee, J. Y. (2023, 24 January). *Systems thinking – the new approach for sustainable and profitable businesses*. Network for Business Sustainability.

[173] McChrystal, G. S., Silverman, D., Collins, T. & Fussell, C. (2015). *Team of teams: new rules of engagement for a complex world*. Penguin.

[174] Derksen M. (2014). Turning men into machines? Scientific management, industrial psychology, and the 'human factor'. *Journal of the History of the Behavioral Sciences*, 50(2):148–165.

[175] Deci, E. L. & Ryan, R. M. (2012). Self-determination theory. In P. A. M. Van Lange, A. W. Kruglanski & E. T. Higgins (eds), *Handbook of theories of social psychology* (pp. 416–437). Sage.

[176] Schiemann, W. A. (2013). From talent management to talent optimization. *Journal of World Business*, 49(2):281–288.

[177] Stanton, N. A., Li, W. & Harris, D. (2017). Ergonomics and human factors in aviation. *Ergonomics*, 60(1):150.

[178] Department of Transport (1990). *Report on the accident to Boeing 737-400 G-OBME near Kegworth, Leicestershire on 8 January 1989* (Aircraft Accident Report 4/90). HMSO.

[179] Duckworth, P. (2020). *Menopause: mind the gap*. HWCS Publications.

[180] Hood, C. & Patton, R. (2021). Exploring the role of psychological need fulfilment on stress, job satisfaction and turnover intention in support

staff working in inpatient mental health hospitals in the NHS: a self-determination theory perspective. *Journal of Mental Health*, 31(5):692–698.

[181] Gagné, M. & Deci, E. L. (2005). Self-determination theory and work motivation. *Journal of Organizational Behavior*, 26(4):331–362.

[182] Ayers, B., Forshaw, M. & Hunter, M. S. (2010b). The impact of attitudes towards the menopause on women's symptom experience: A systematic review. *Maturitas*, 65(1):28–36.

[183] British Menopause Society (2022). *Cognitive Behaviour Therapy (CBT) for menopausal symptoms*. In Women's Health Concern.

[184] Sprague, J. & Hayes, J. (2000). Self-determination and empowerment: a feminist standpoint analysis of talk about disability. *American Journal of Community Psychology*, 28(5):671–695.

[185] Seibert, S. E., Silver, S. R. & Randolph, W. A. (2004). Taking empowerment to the next level: a multiple-level model of empowerment, performance, and satisfaction. *Academy of Management Journal*, 47(3):332–349.

[186] Benoit, Ilgim, Foreman, Jeffrey R and Guy, Bonnie S. (2024). Person-supervisor fit antecedents: Self-Determination Theory in salesforce turnover intention, *Atlantic Marketing Journal*, 3(1).

[187] Ju, D., Ma, L., Ren, R. & Zhang, Y. (2019). Empowered to break the silence: applying self-determination theory to employee silence. *Frontiers in Psychology*, 10.

[188] Gagné, M., Parker, S. K., Griffin, M. A., Dunlop, P. D., Knight, C., Klonek, F. E. & Parent-Rocheleau, X. (2022). Understanding and shaping the future of work with self-determination theory. *Nature Reviews Psychology*, 1(7):378–392.

[189] Ahearne, M., Mathieu, J. & Rapp, A. (2005). To empower or not to empower your sales force? An empirical examination of the influence of leadership empowerment behavior on customer satisfaction and performance. *Journal of Applied Psychology*, 90(5):945–955.

[190] Manganelli, L., Thibault-Landry, A., Forest, J. & Carpentier, J. (2018). Self-Determination Theory can help you generate performance and well-being in the workplace: a review of the literature. *Advances in Developing Human Resources*, 20(2):227–240.

[191] Deci, E. L. & Ryan, R. M. (2012). Self-Determination Theory. In P. A. M. Van Lange, A. W. Kruglanski & E. T. Higgins (eds), *Handbook of theories of social psychology* (pp. 416–437). Sage.

¹⁹² Manganelli, L., Thibault-Landry, A., Forest, J. & Carpentier, J. (2018). Self-Determination Theory can help you generate performance and well-Being in the workplace: a review of the literature. *Advances in Developing Human Resources*, 20(2):227–240.

¹⁹³ Spence, G. B. & Oades, L. G. (2011). Coaching with self-determination in mind: using theory to advance evidence-based coaching practice. *DOAJ (DOAJ: Directory of Open Access Journals)*.

¹⁹⁴ Spreitzer, G. M. (1995). Psychological empowerment in the workplace: dimensions, measurement, and validation. *Academy of Management Journal*, 38(5):1442–1465.

¹⁹⁵ Durham, P. (2024, 6 March). *'Empowerment' key to managing menopause.* Medical Republic.

¹⁹⁶ Hickey, M., LaCroix, A. Z., Doust, J., Mishra, G. D., Sivakami, M., Garlick, D. & Hunter, M. S. (2024). An empowerment model for managing menopause. *The Lancet*, 403(10430):947–957.

¹⁹⁷ Verburgh, M., Verdonk, P., Appelman, Y., Zanten, M. B. & Nieuwenhuijsen, K. (2020). 'I get that spirit in me' – mentally empowering workplace health promotion for female workers in low-paid jobs during menopause and midlife. *International Journal of Environmental Research and Public Health*, 17(18):6462.

¹⁹⁸ Doubova, S. V., Espinosa-Alarcón, P., Flores-Hernández, S., Infante, C. & Pérez-Cuevas, R. (2011). Integrative health care model for climacteric stage women: design of the intervention. *BMC Women S Health*, 11(1).

¹⁹⁹ Kafaei-Atrian, M., Sadat, Z., Nasiri, S. & Izadi-Avanji, F. S. (2022). The effect of self-care education based on self- theory, individual empowerment model, and their integration on quality of life among menopausal women. *DOAJ (DOAJ: Directory of Open Access Journals)*, 10(1):54–63.

²⁰⁰ Yun, H., Kim, C., Ahn, J. & Schlenk, E. A. (2023). Effects of a self-determination theory-based physical activity programme for postmenopausal women with rheumatoid arthritis: A randomized controlled trial. *International Journal of Nursing Practice*, 29(6).

²⁰¹ Sprague, J. & Hayes, J. (2000). Self-determination and empowerment: a feminist standpoint analysis of talk about disability. *American Journal of Community Psychology*, 28(5):671–695.

²⁰² Dunn, S. (2022). The experience of workplace coaching for menopausal women: a descriptive phenomenological study (Academic Paper). *International Journal of Evidence Based Coaching and Mentoring*, 97–108.

[203] Hardy, C., Griffiths, A. & Hunter, M. S. (2017). What do working menopausal women want? A qualitative investigation into women's perspectives on employer and line manager support. *Maturitas*, 101:37–41.

[204] Zhou, H. & Chen, J. (2021). How does psychological empowerment prevent emotional exhaustion? Psychological safety and organizational embeddedness as mediators. *Frontiers in Psychology*, 12.

[205] Allan, I., Ammi, M. & Dedewanou, F. A. (2024). The impact of sense of belonging on health: Canadian evidence. *Applied Economics*, 1–13. From: https://doi.org/10.1080/00036846.2024.2364075

[206] Virgin Media O2. Gender-pay-gap-report_master_v12.2024.

[207] British Standards Institute (n.d.). *Strengthening menopause policies at Virgin Media O2*. BSI Insights.

[208] McBurnie (2024, September) J. *Mental health investment across your organisation. Proving, measuring and monitoring support. Learning from a menopause clinic* (Keynote). Westminster Insight. Menopause in the Workplace Conference, UK.

[209] Unum & O'Donnell, P. (2014). *The cost of turnover*. Oxford Economics.

[210] Bawa, V. (2024, September). *Elevate your business: retaining talent with better menopause at work policies* (Keynote panel discussion). Westminster Insight. Menopause in the Workplace Conference, UK.

[211] Women in Tech (2024, 6 August). *Embracing inclusivity: BAE systems' support for menopause in the workplace*.

[212] https://helptogrow.campaign.gov.uk/empowering-menopause-support-workplace-inclusivity-at-holland-barrett/

[213] #TimeForChange: BVA launches new menopause hub to support members and help keep highly-skilled vets in the profession (2023). *Politics Home*.

[214] Chung, H. (2022). *The flexibility paradox: why flexible working leads to (self-) exploitation*. Policy Press.

[215] Zurich UK (2024, 5 April). Zurich quadruples part time hires in just five years as it shows commitment to the Flexible Working Act. From: Zurich.co.uk

[216] Zurich UK (2022, 15 February). Zurich rolls out menopause training for 700 managers. From: Zurich.co.uk

[217] Goldin, C. (2023). Gender pay gap? Culprit is 'greedy work.' *The Harvard Gazette*.

[218] Cooban, A. (2022, 19 October). Bank of Ireland offers workers paid menopause leave. *CNN.*

[219] O'Sullivan, S. (2023). *My life on pause.* Olympia Publishers.

[220] *Menopause Workplace Pledge* (n.d.). WellbeingofWomen.org.

[221] Unilever (2022, 14 October). *Unilever UK & Ireland recognised as a menopause friendly employer.*

[222] Nosek, B. (2019, 11 June). *Strategy for Culture Change.* Center for Open Science.

[223] Furby, L. (2023, 11 October). Making menopause normal at Specsavers. *Optometry Today.*

[224] Furby, L. (2024, September). *The role of menopause champions in a new framework for global menopause initiatives* (Keynote). Westminster Insight. Menopause in the Workplace Conference, UK.

[225] Harlow, S. D., Burnett-Bowie, S. A. M., Greendale, G. A. et al. (2022). Disparities in reproductive aging and midlife health between black and white women: the Study of Women's Health Across the Nation (SWAN). *Womens Midlife Health*, 8:3.

[226] British Occupational Hygiene Society & Chartered Society for Worker Health Protection. (2023b). *Uncovering the UK's hidden crisis in women's workplace health* (p. 1).

[227] Health and Safety Executive. (n.d.). *Musculoskeletal disorders at work.* From: www.hse.gov.uk.

[228] Wright, V. J., Schwartzman, J. D., Itinoche, R. & Wittstein, J. (2024). The musculoskeletal syndrome of menopause. *Climacteric*, 1–7. From: https://doi.org/10.1080/13697137.2024.2380363

[229] www.networkrail.co.uk/stories/network-rail-recognised-as-the-times-top-50-employers-for-gender-equality/

[230] https://rise.articulate.com/share/mO8V7QtSs2ZXzpUT3iNbvId2s3ZE4iDj#/

[231] Pearsall, H. (2024, September). *Elevate your business: Retaining talent with better menopause at work policies* [Keynote Panel Discussion]. Westminster Insight. Menopause in the Workplace Conference, UK.

[232] Hays plc. (2023). Strategic report. In *Hays plc Annual Report & Accounts.* haysplc.com

Useful resources

Professional and not-for-profit bodies supporting organizations

ACAS:	www.acas.org.uk/menopause-at-work
BSI:	www.bsigroup.com
CIPD:	www.cipd.org/uk/topics/menopause
Fawcett Society:	www.fawcettsociety.org.uk/ menopause and the workplace
UK Government Help to Grow:	helptogrow.campaign.gov.uk/ menopause-and-the-workplace/

Medical information and support

Balance App, Menopause Library and Masterclass:	www.drlouisenewson.co.uk
British Menopause Society:	www.thebms.org.uk
International Menopause Society:	www.imsociety.org
Menopause Matters:	www.menopausematters.co.uk
NHS guidance on menopause:	www.nhs.uk/conditions/menopause
NICE guidelines:	www.nice.org.uk/guidance/ng23
Women's Health Concern:	www.womens-health-concern.org

Inclusive menopause support

Black women in Menopause:	www.blackhealthandbeyond.co.uk
Daisy Network – premature menopause:	www.daisynetwork.org
Queer menopause:	www.queermenopause.com/resources
Rock my Menopause – transgender:	https//:rockmymenopause.com/get-informed/transgender-health/

Acknowledgements

Writing this book has been my 'Everest'. My whole career I have set my sights on conquering that peak; aspiring to stick my professional flag somewhere challenging and important; taking a real-life problem where no one has quite gone with it before.

This year [2024], a gap in the clouds emerged and I took the chance. It has been a mission, requiring months of grit and focus. And it has been a joy, to indulge in something I love and which I care passionately about. However, while this has been a deeply personal journey, no expedition would be possible without an amazing back-up crew.

I'd like to say thank you to all those who have inspired and walked alongside me. Not least of these is Alison Jones and her team at Practical Inspiration Publishing (PIP), whose reassuring but laser-focused guidance showed the way.

A huge thank you to the people who woke me up to the possibilities: my friend Rachel Oliver who kept pressing me to use my skills in the menopause space – I got there in the end!; all the female warriors in my life with their own stories and incredible friendship; medical expert Louise Newson, whose menopause podcasts have kept me company these last few years and from whom I have learned so much; Davina McCall, legend that she is, who helped me face my own barriers to talking about women's stuff. And also thanks to my brother Steve Andrews who I have been watching and learning from in his own writing journey, and who has bravely put up with me rushing past him towards publication (sorry Steve)!

For the content, a massive thank you to the experts who helped to fact check my earlier drafts: Heidi Cooper at HCR Law for her review of employment law on menopause; Dr. Clair Crocket at Newson Health; and Dr. Celia Cotton, private GP and member of the British Menopause Society for their thoughtful reviews of the medical-related information; and Adam Haycock for his critical review of the gender and socio-political aspects in the book.

Next, can I give a big shout out for my generous alpha and beta-draft reviewers: Katie Stokes for her brilliant early thoughts, encouragement and suggestions on structure, language and tone, and her willingness to read it all again at the next stage; Alli Trott for her careful reading of the book and suggestions from a practitioner, and fellow writer, perspective; and to the editing team at PIP who helped me to move it up another level.

I extend a special thank you to all the case study contributors who gave their time freely to support this project: Vicky Bawa at BAE Systems; Jacqui McBurnie for the NHS; Steve Collinson at Zurich UK; Lou Furby at Specsavers; Gill Graham at Cargyll; Sarah Grainger and Elizabeth Warner at West Mercia Police; Joanne Healey at Bank of Ireland; Hannah Lacey at the BVA; Sam Marshall-Keith and Emma Taylor at Dean Close Foundation; Network Rail; Siobhan O'Sullivan author of *My Life on Pause*; Rachel Pearce at Unilever; Hannah Pearsall at Hays; Clare Stafford at Holland and Barrett; Virgin Media O2; Maxine Zaidman at JBA Consulting. Plus Maxine Fletcher at Oxford Brookes University for sharing her practical experience.

Finally, thank you to my wonderful crew: my parents John and Jean Andrews for passing on a love of writing, and for their unquestioning support on all things, including this book (as dad said to me, 'If it feels uncomfortable, then it means it's worth doing'); my sons Doug, Adam and Toby for the laughs, the pride and the adventures that got me through my rocky menopause years; and (don't worry, I haven't forgotten you!) Richard Robins for his unfailing care, positivity, fun and practicality that made all the difference in keeping me going – I think it's time we went on another holiday, love!

Index

Note: page numbers in *italic* type refer to figures; those in **bold** type refer to tables.

A
ACAS (Advisory, Conciliation and Arbitration Service), UK xx
adaptation, women's capacity for 148–151
adrenaline 27
African Caribbean women 27, 30, 173
age, discrimination claims on the grounds of 60, 61, 62
ageing workforce 3, 4–6
alcohol consumption 39
allies 167
andropause 32
antidepressants 36
anxiety 36, 77, 81, 137, 138, 151, 173, 175
attraction of talent xix, 50–51, 189
aviation industry 90–91

B
BAE Systems 117
Bank of Ireland 143
beliefs, negative 152–155
biopsychosocial lens on menopause xxii–xiii
blood sugar levels 39
BOHS (British Occupational Hygiene Society) 87
brain fog 14, 36, 151, 153, 175, 179
brand reputation and value 54–55, 113
breast cancer, and HRT 41, 42
breath control 39
BSI Standard, 'menstruation, menstrual health and menopause in the workplace' 111
business case for menopause-friendly strategies xix–xx, 49–50, 72, 108, 111–114, 125
BVA (British Veterinary Association) 129–130

C
Cahn, N. 63
career progression 45, *47*, 190
Cargyll 151
caring responsibilities 13, 14
 sandwich generation 15
CBT (cognitive behavioural therapy) 39, 93, 153
Channel 4 45
CIPD (Chartered Institute of Personnel and Development) xx, 4, 5, 35, 44–45
coaching 94, 95, 117, 135, 151, 153, 167, 168, 188, 190, 192
cognitive symptoms 36–37, *38*, 80, 137
communication
 advocacy 120, 123, 136, 153
 conversations on menopause xx, 74, 77, 82, 105, 120, 121, 130, 167, 168, 180
 listening to women and their experiences 127–130
 menopause awareness and skills 158–161
 see also openness (M-POWERED framework)
community 165–169

competence/effectiveness 94, 97
confidence 148, 149
see also effectiveness (M-POWERED framework)
Conservative Government xx
consultation 115
control/agency, loss of 134, 196
   autonomy/control 94, 96–97, 134
   see also will (M-POWERED framework)
cortisol 27
Covid-19 pandemic 5, 20–21, 111
Credit Suisse Research 53
CSR (corporate social responsibility) 54
cultural, ethnic and racial diversity 27, 30, 37–38, 41, 173
culture change 161–164, 185

D
Dean Close Foundation 187
Deci, E. L. 94
decision-making
   informed 96
   shared 134–136
deliverables, flexing of 141–143
delivery (M-POWERED framework) **104**, 184–194
depression 36, 77, 81
desk fans 87, 87, 92, 173, 174, 197
dietary changes 39
disability
   discrimination claims on the grounds of 59, 60, 61, 62, 63, 66, 142
   equal pay legislation 64
   reasonable adjustments 67, 68–69, 172
discrimination
   ageism 78
   'combined' (dual) 64
   direct/indirect 65
   legal issues 59, 60
   see also employment protection legislation
distributive justice 57
diversity *see* EDI (equity, diversity and inclusion) strategies
divorce 13, 16
doctors, menopause training and awareness 43, 74–75

E
early menopause 31–32
economic growth, national 22
economic inactivity, pre-retirement age 6
   government policies, and women's economic activity 22

EDI (equity, diversity and inclusion) strategies 54–59, *58*, 188
effectiveness (M-POWERED framework) **104**, 148–156, 192
EHRC (Equality and Human Rights Commission), UK 69
emotional symptoms 36, *38*, 80
employment, impact of menopause on 44–47, *45*, 47
employment legislation xx
   Employment Rights Act 1996 60, 69
   UK 60–63, 64–72
   USA 63–64
employment policies 188
   see also attraction; progression; recruitment; retention; talent optimization
employment tribunal cases
   A. vs Bonmarche Ltd 2019 67
   Best vs Embark on Raw Ltd 2006 66–67
   Coleman vs Bobby Dodd Institute 2017 64
   Davies vs Scottish Courts and Tribunal Service 2018 68–69
   Farquharson vs Thistle Marine 2023 67
   Lynskey vs Direct Line Insurance Services 2022 66
   Rooney vs Leicester City Council 2021 63
   Shearer vs South Lanarkshire Council 2023 71
empowerment 93–96, 155
   psychological empowerment 134
empty nest 16
environment (M-POWERED framework) **104**, 172–181, 192
equality 57–58
equity 57
   see also EDI (equity, diversity and inclusion) strategies
ethical payoff of menopause-friendly strategies 50, *52*, 54–59, *55*, *58*
exercise 39
exit 190
external experts/groups, role of 167–168

F
families, prosperity of 22
fans 87, *87*, 92, 173, 174, 197
Fawcett Society 45, 46, 80, 81
finance sector, female workforce 51
financial payoff of menopause-friendly strategies 50–59, *52*, *58*
financial security, as motivation to work 10

Index | 225

First World War 19–20
flexible working 6, 137–143, 188
   employers' right to refuse 143–145
   from first day of employment 69–70
forgetfulness 36
Frostrup, Mariella xviii

G
Gen X women 9, 15
gender dysmorphia 32
gender pay gap *11*, 11–13, *12*, 111, 141
gender reassignment, discrimination claims on the grounds of 61, 62
genitourinary problems 35
Gilbreth, Lillian and Frank 88
'greedy work' 141
growth mindset 148–151
gut health 39

H
habits, negative 152–155
harassment 66–67
Hays 190–191
health and safety at work 71–72, 172, 177–180
health issues, older workforce 5–6
healthcare provision, menopause symptoms 43
healthcare sector, female workforce 51
Henpicked 'Menopause-Friendly Employer' accreditation 110
Hickey, M. 95
HM Courts and Tribunal Service 60
Holland & Barrett 124
hormonal changes, menopause transition 26–33, *30*, *31*, 82–84
hot flushes 34, 35, 37, 137, 172, 173–175, 178, 196
hours, flexing of 139–141
household responsibilities 14–15
HRT (hormone replacement therapy) 33, 40–43, 97
HSE (Health and Safety Executive) 71
human factors 90
humour, inappropriate 81, *81*
hybrid working 20, 70
   home, working from 137–139
hydration 39, 172, 174, 178

I
IFS 10, 12
impact on employment 44–47, *45*, *47*
inclusion *see* EDI (equity, diversity and inclusion) strategies
Indian women 30

industrialization, and changing work patterns 18
insulin resistance 27
interactional justice 56
invisibility, of older women 76–79, 86
Invisible Women (Perez) 86
IT and technology sectors, female workforce 51

J
Jaguar Land Rover 53–54
JBA Consulting 154–155

K
Kegworth air accident, 1989 91

L
Labour Government xx, 64
legal issues 59–72, *61*, 164
life expectancy 4, 5–6
lifestyle changes 39

M
male hormone decline 29, 32–33
McCall, Davina xviii
meaning/purpose 96
melatonin 37
menopause terminology
   biopsychosocial lens xxii–xiii
   as a global issue xxiii–xxiv
   as a process xxii
   terminology xxii
menopause action plans, delivery of 184–194
menopause audit 192–193
menopause awareness and skills 158–161
menopause champions, role of xx, 166
menopause-friendly culture 161–164
menopause-friendly working environment 172–181
menopause 'golden thread' 187–191
menopause inequity 125–127
menopause networks 165
menopause penalty 3–4, *11*, 11–13, *12*
menopause policy 116
Menopause Risk Assessment tool, West Mercia Police 174–175
menopause symptoms 33–34, *35*, *38*
   cognitive symptoms 36–37, 80, 137
   cultural and ethnic diversity 37–38
   emotional symptoms 36, 80
   interaction between 37
   physical symptoms 35, 79–82, *81*
   see also HRT (hormone replacement therapy)

226 | M-POWER

menopause symptoms management 33–34, 35, 38
  management of 33, 97
  medical management 43
  non-medical management 39, 97
  menopause terminology
menopause terminology
  for trans and non-binary people xxiii, 32, 62
Menopause Toolkit, Network Rail 180
menopause transition 25–26
  hormonal changes 26–33, 30, 31
  menopause 29–30
  perimenopause xxii, 15, 29, 33, 34, 37
  post-menopause xxii, 30
  sudden or early menopause 31–32
  see also menopause symptoms
menstruation, bleeding issues 35, 79–80, 172, 176–177
mental health 36, 179
merit 57
midlife losses 16
mindfulness 39
monitoring progress 191–193
motherhood penalty 12
M-POWERED framework xvii, xx, 103–104, **104**, 192, 196
  Brew People xxi, 155
musculo-skeletal disorders 35, 178

N
National Child Development Survey 46
negative beliefs, emotions and habits 152–155
Network Rail 180
Newson Health 33, 34, 36, 52
NHS, cost of menopause to 51
NHS, North East and North Cumbria 111–112
night sweats 35

O
occupational disease 86–87
occupational health policy 188
OECD 6, 7
oestrogen 29, 31, 42
  HRT (hormone replacement therapy) 40
  as a male hormone 28
Office for National Statistics, UK 14
older women 4–6, 189, 196
  cultural invisibility of 76–79
  demographics 3
  employment rates xix, 7, 7–10, 8, 9, 195
  financial insecurity 13
  health issues 6

as key focus xxiii
listening to experiences of 127–130
motivation to work 10–11, 22–23
negative stereotypes of 77
positive narratives around 79, 79
terminology xxiii, 77
wider life challenges 13, 13–16
see also women
onboarding 189
openness (M-POWERED framework) **104**, 120–131, 192
organizational culture
  culture change 161–164, 185
  inappropriate humour 81, 81
organizational justice 56–58, 58
organizational performance 109
organizations, strategic drivers around menopause 109–110
O'Sullivan, Siobhan 152

P
Palermo, G. 10
participation 109, 126
part-time work 12, 14, 46
  flexing hours 139–141
PCOS (polycystic ovary syndrome) 27
pension ages, rise in 5, 6, 10
pension pay gap, UK 13
people managers, role of 166–167
Perez, Caroline 86
performance 52–54, 109, 126
performance management 149, 188, 190
perimenopause xxii, 15, 29, 33, 34, 37
personal fulfilment, as motivation to work 10
Pew Research Center 14
physical working environment 69, 71, 92, 93, 121, 134, 172
  menopause-friendly 172–181
  see also work design
physical symptoms 35, 38, 79–82, 81
planning, for delivery of menopause action plans 184–194
positive mindset 93
post-menopause xxii, 30
procedural justice 56
productivity 110
progesterone 29, 31, 42
  HRT (hormone replacement therapy) 40
progress monitoring 191–193
progression 4, 13, 34, 44, 45, 47, 109, 127, 155, 190
project management 185–186
  'agile' 185–186
psychological strategies 93

Index | 227

psychological support 39
psychosis 33
public toilets 84–86, *85*
purpose (M-POWERED framework) **104**, 108–118, 192

R

race
  discrimination claims on the grounds of 61
  equal pay legislation 64
  see also ethnic diversity, and menopause
reasonable adjustments 67, 68–69, 172
recruitment 111
  costs 51, 113
redundancy 190
relatedness 94, 98
relationships (M-POWERED framework) **104**, 157–170, 192
reputational risk, legal issues 59
resistance to menopause action plans 164
resources risk, legal issues 59
retail sector, female workforce 51
retention xix, 50–51, 111, 189
retirement ages, increase in 5, 6
risk assessments, health and safety issues 178, 180
ROI (return on investment) 108, 112–114, 193
role models, positive 151–152
Ryan, R. M. 94

S

sales delivery 110
sandwich generation 15
sanitary care facilities 172, 176–177
SDT (Self Determination Theory) 94
Second World War 19
self-employment 6
senior leadership, role of 166
senior roles, underrepresentation of women in 52–53, 111
sexual orientation, discrimination claims on the grounds of 61
shareholder value 110
silence, around menopause 73–76, *76*
'silent ceiling' 73
single parents 16, 22
sleep disorders 35, 37, 179
social care sector, female workforce 51
social isolation 138
social obligations/commitments 110
social return on investment 54, 110
specialist coaches, role of 167

Specsavers 168–169
Spreitzer, G. M. 95
SROI (social return on investment) 54, 110
stakeholder engagement 114–118, 193
strategic alignment 108–112
strategic payoff of menopause-friendly strategies 50–59, *52*, *58*
strengths, focus on 148–151
stress
  hormonal impact 27
  workplace environment adaptations 175
sudden menopause 31–32
suicide 112
  suicide intentionality 33, 36
systems-thinking approach 87, 88, 187
  aviation industry 90–91
  and menopause 92

T

taboo around menopause xix, xviii, 74, 80, 83, 96, 110, 120, 166, 192, 196
talent optimization xix, 52–54
Taylor, Frederick/Taylorism 88, 89–90
teaching sector, female workforce 51
temperature 172, 173–175
testosterone 27, 29, *31*
  and the andropause 32–33
  as a female hormone 28
  HRT (hormone replacement therapy) 40
thriving 109, 127
training and development 116, 190
  costs 51
  menopause awareness and skills 158–161, 163

U

unfair dismissal 60
uniform requirements, flexing of 173
  safety critical clothing 180
Unilever 159–160
USA
  employment protection legislation 63–64
  women's employment rates 7
  women's unpaid work 14

V

ventilation 174
Virgin Media O2 110–111

W

West Mercia Police 174–175
WHI (Women's Health Initiative) 41, 42

will (M-POWERED framework) **104**, 134–146, 192
women
  car-buying decisions 53–54
  Covid-19 pandemic and home working 20
  life expectancy 6
  listening to experiences of 127–130
  personal drivers of 109
  retirement age, increase in 5, 6, 10
  unpaid work 14–15
  see also older women
women of colour
  ageism 78
  menopausal symptoms 27
women-only events 165
work
  evolution of and impact for women 17–20
  women's changing relationship with 20–21
  women's employment rates xix, 7, 7–10, *8*, *9*
work design 84, 86–92
  public toilets 84–86, *85*
  see also physical working environment
work location, flexibility of 137–139
working from home 137–139

Y
yoga 39
YouGov 54

Z
Zurich 141

A quick word from Practical Inspiration Publishing…

We hope you found this book both practical and inspiring – that's what we aim for with every book we publish.

We publish titles on topics ranging from leadership, entrepreneurship, HR and marketing to self-development and wellbeing.

Find details of all our books at: www.practicalinspiration.com

 Did you know…

We can offer discounts on bulk sales of all our titles – ideal if you want to use them for training purposes, corporate giveaways or simply because you feel these ideas deserve to be shared with your network.

We can even produce bespoke versions of our books, for example with your organization's logo and/or a tailored foreword.

To discuss further, contact us on info@practicalinspiration.com.

 Got an idea for a business book?

We may be able to help. Find out more about publishing in partnership with us at: bit.ly/PIpublishing.

Follow us on social media…

- @PIPTalking
- @pip_talking
- @practicalinspiration
- @piptalking
- Practical Inspiration Publishing